Follow Our Lady
Star of the Sea
She leads us to her Son.

pray for
Bobby

Kay West, 2012

# Star of the Sea

## a history of
## The Basilica
## St. Mary Star of the Sea

by Bob J. Bernreuter

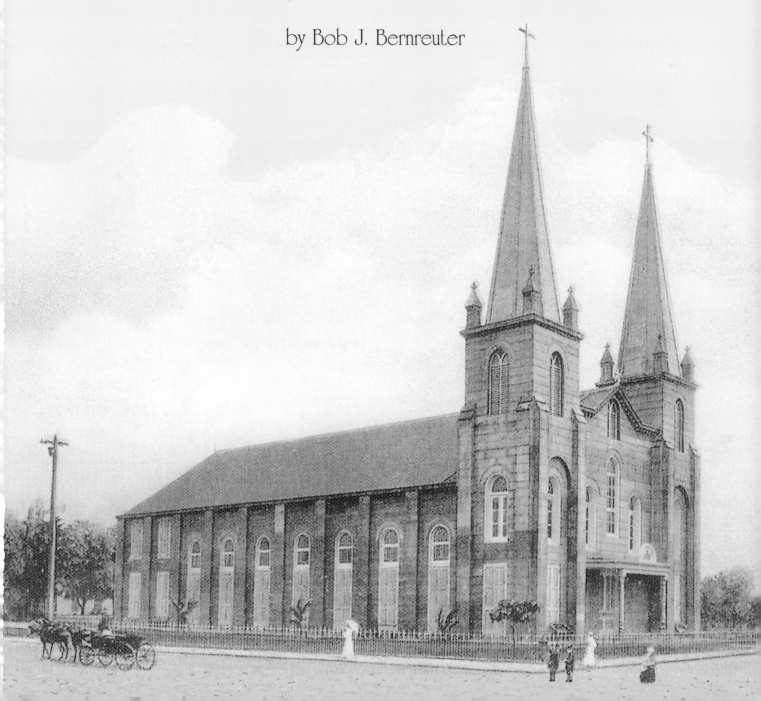

161676

St. Mary Star of the Sea collection

AMERICAN HISTORY STUDENTS DISPLAY HISTORICAL RELICS FROM THE SPANISH AMERICAN WAR—Elsie and Davie hold up the thirty-eight starred flag flown atop the battleship Maine when it was sunk in Habana Harbor. Susie displays one of its signal flags. Carolyn holds a box of hardtack—still edible! *Seated*—Conchita holds a pair of ankle cuffs from the brig of some American ship; Beatrice has the hospital records of those treated at C. M. I. hospital in 1898; Aida holds one of the battle-flags. Netta and Lucille, seated behind the wheel of the Maine, hold shattered pieces of the ship. 1948

Key West Publishing, LLC
FAX: 305-296-7386
E-mail: keywestpubLLC@aol.com
www. keywestpublishingllc.com

Star of the Sea
© Copyright 2012 Bob J. Bernreutrer

Library of Congress Control Number: 2012907728
Library of Congress Cataloging-in-Publication Data

Bernreuter, Bob J. (Bob Joseph)
 Star of the sea : a history of the Basilica St. Mary Star of the Sea / by Bob J. Bernreuter.
    p. cm.
 Includes bibliographical references (p.     ).
 ISBN 978-0-9778528-4-0 (alk. paper)
 1. Basilica St. Mary Star of the Sea (Key West, Fla.)--History. 2. Key West (Fla.)--Church history. 3. Catholic Church--Florida--Key West--History. I. Title.
 BX4781.K49B47 2012
 282'.75941--dc23
                              2012029277

Printed in USA
CPSIA: 1-2000-12-37040

# *Mary, Star of Hope*

With a hymn composed in the eighth or ninth century, thus for over a thousand years, the Church has greeted Mary, the Mother of God, as "Star of the Sea": Ave Maris Stella. Human life is a journey. Towards what destination? How do we find the way? Life is like a voyage on the sea of history, often dark and stormy, a voyage in which we watch for the stars that indicate the route. The true stars of our life are the people who have lived good lives. They are lights of hope. Certainly, Jesus Christ is the true light, the sun that has risen above all the shadows of history. But to reach him we also need lights close by—people who shine with his light and so guide us along our way. Who more than Mary could be a star of hope for us? With her "yes" she opened the door of our world to God himself; she became the living Ark of the Covenant, in whom God took flesh, became one of us, and pitched his tent among us (cf. Jn 1:14).

**...**

Star of the Sea, shine upon us
and guide us on our way!

**Pope Benedict XVI**
**From his Encyclical Letter, *Spe Salvi***

St. Peter
The Keys to the Kingdom

St. Paul
The sword of persecution

The Gospel of Matthew
Jesus the Lion of Juda

These are the Icons over the Sanctuary and what they represent.

The Gospel of Mark
Jesus the Ox of Action

The Gospel of Luke
Jesus the Man for his Humanity

The Gospel of John
Jesus the Eagle for his Divinity

The Eucharist

The Holy Spirit

# *Our Pastor's Introduction*
## Built on a Rock

"Everyone who listens to these words of mine and acts on them will be like a wise man who built his house on rock. The rain fell, the floods came, and the winds blew and buffeted the house. But it did not collapse; it had been set solidly on rock." Matthew 7:24-25

Key West's quintessential geography and geology facilitated human habitation long before habitation in the other Keys, in any other place in the Archdiocese of Miami, and in most of Florida.

The Florida Keys are a narrow, gently curving chain of sub-tropical islands extending one hundred and thirteen miles from the tip of Florida to Key West which is ninety miles north of Havana, Cuba. "Key" comes from the Spanish word, 'Cayo' which means Small Island.

To the south and to the east of Key West and the Florida Keys is the Atlantic Ocean which is held in check by the third largest coral reef in the world. This coral reef provides a natural harbor from the confluence of capricious ocean and sea currents and streams which have directed many to Key West willingly, and sometimes unwillingly, from the Atlantic Ocean, the Gulf of Mexico and the Florida Straits.

Unique to Key West is its geology of oolitic lime stone in the surface, deep below the surface and rising above the surface to 16 feet above sea level. The perfect host for wells and cisterns to collect rain water; the porous oolite also protects the wells from ocean saline and bacteria, rendering reserves of potable water. The providence of God's creation in the unique geography and geology of Key West and the lower Keys provided a viable dwelling for His creatures and thus stability for the development of peoples and for the propagation of faith.

The present Saint Mary Star of the Sea Church is literally built upon, and built from, this oolitic limestone rock. The Church building is of concrete made from an aggregate of limestone dug from the grounds and beach sand which is of coral. Although the furnishings and the statuary within the Church have suffered through the ravages of time, tropical weather, and termites, Saint Mary Star of the Sea Church stands firmly upon this rock and most importantly, upon the rock of Saint Peter.

Rev. John C. Baker
Rector

HOLY * HOLY * HOLY
is written above
the tabernacle door depicting
The Annunciation
of the
Archangel Gabriel
to the
Blessed Virgin Mary
with the presence of the Holy Spirit

The inscription in Latin is from John 1:14
**ET VERBVM CARO FACTVM EST**

AND THE WORD WAS MADE FLESH

Behind this sacred door are the words that I trust will bring
the history of St. Mary Star of the Sea Parish to life.

Picture depicts church with original portico

# Star of the Sea
## A history of the Basilica
## St. Mary Star of the Sea,
## the oldest Roman Catholic Parish
## in South Florida

To the many priests, sisters, and brothers, who dedicated their lives to proclaim the gospel of Jesus Christ in Key West.

To the men and women of this parish who endured innumerable hardships and maintained their devotion to the spreading of the Catholic faith.

To the community of Key West which through the centuries highly esteemed and supported the endeavors of our Catholic Religious on the island.

This history is dedicated to their memory.

# *Acknowledgments*

First and foremost, I must give credit to Sister Mary Pat Vandercar, who helped immensely during the original compilation of the church's history. Her tireless efforts in contacting and obtaining early records from the different archives of all the dioceses to which Key West has belonged enabled us to put together a list of many, if not most, of the priests and nuns who have served the island.

To Father Eugene Quinlan for his enthusiasm, encouragement, and inspiration which initiated the first history of St. Mary Star of the Sea.

To Father Gerald F. McGrath for his support which enabled the completion of the first history.

To Archbishop Thomas Wenski who recognized the spiritual and historical contributions of our parish to the Catholic faith in South Florida, the architectural significance of our Church, and therefore successfully petitioned the Vatican to recognize and distinguish St. Mary Star of the Sea with the title of Minor Basilica.

To Father John C. Baker, who contributed documents, research, and unfettered access to the church's resources, which enabled this edition of the history to be as rich as it is. His consultations, advice, and patience have been a guiding light to me and a reflection of the spirituality of our parish.

To Fr. Michael J. McNally, Catholic author and historian, for his review, suggestions, and corrections of the work. His published histories of Catholicism in South Florida were a great reference source for a large part of this book.

To my wife Iris for her encouragement, patience, and proofreading during this process.

To George and Georgina Ruffing, who contributed in so many ways to the history.

To Sue Barroso for her help in research, editing, and proofreading the book.

To Tom Hambright, local historian of the Monroe County Library for all his assistance.

To Ray Blazevic for his additions and critique of this work.

To Bob Wolz, Director of Truman's Little White House, for help in locating photos.

To Suellen Croteau for meticulously editing the final edition of this work.

To Ursula W. Elliot who collected the stories of St. Francis Xavier School's students.

To Sr. Dolores Wehle, and Sr. Theresa Cecilia (Birdie) Lowe for help with Sisters of the Holy Names history.

To Fr. Vincent Orlando and the Jesuit Archivists for finding photos of priests.

To Fr. Arthur Dennison for his editing and suggestions.

To Tom Oosterhoudt for use of many of his photos.

To all the parishioners of St. Mary Star of the Sea, who have brought forth articles, information on ministries, and reminded me of important events: Nancy Cooper, Ida Roberts, Kathy Kolhage, Rose Thomas, Kathy Roberts, Beth Harris, Charles and Nelia Malby Sr., Charles Malby Jr., Ralph Henriquez, Tony Herce, Angela McClain, and Deacon Peter Batty.

To the many I am sure I have left out. So many people contributed to this huge undertaking and to each I wish to express my gratitude and thanks.

# Table of Contents

# The Name

Exactly when, or even who first named the island of Key West remains unknown. The aboriginal natives had a name for the islands they inhabited, to them our island was known as Cuchiyaga, but that name failed to survive the passing of time and cultures. The origin of "Key" to define a small island is thought to be a derivation of "Cayo", not originally a Spanish word, but a word they may have adapted from the Taino Indians of Cuba.

The legend of our island's history tells the tale of early Spanish explorers landing on our island and finding the beaches strewn with bones. Many Florida Indian cultures did not bury their dead, rather they would remove the flesh from the bones by leaving them out in the open, and when they were dry they would gather them up and place them in a box to be honored. Some say the bones were remnants of a great Indian war, while some claim they were only turtle bones, and yet others insist it wasn't the bones at all, but a seven year apple tree which existed on the island and known by the Spanish as "hueso". Whichever it was, we know the name "Cayo Hueso", which translated means "Bone Key" or "Island of Bones", was the first recorded name used for the island and is still used today by Spanish cultures.

The English used "Cay" to describe small islands, such as those in the Bahamas and pronounce it "key", while Americans would pronounce this as the letter "K". It was the English who corrupted the Spanish sounding "Cayo Hueso" to "Key West", either because of the "Hueso" sound, or because it is the western most of the chain of islands, therefore Key West.

# Foreword

Catholicity in South Florida was formalized on Dec. 8, 1852, with the founding of St. Mary Star of the Sea parish, the third oldest Catholic Parish in Florida. A parish is more than a church building; it is more than the clergy, the staff, lay ministries, and parishioners. A parish is all of that and much more. It is part of a community and in a different way the community becomes part of the parish.

This story could be told in many ways. One could separate the history of each entity within the parish: the buildings, the schools, the religious, the people, even the ministries. I have chosen to tell the story of our parish first within its chronological order and secondly within the context of the larger community.

What is this parish's community? At first glance it seems simply to float upon the seas with no care to the rest of the world. However, in examining our history, we see that this concept is far from the truth. This island community floats upon the seas of a much larger world whose waves rock us and shock us. This is also a world that desperately needs us.

Remarkably the 1890 census showed Key West as the largest city in Florida. By 1900 the city's population had grown to 16,000, while a hundred and fifty miles to the north only 1,700 people called Miami home. The island's proximity to Cuba during the early Spanish occupation, its natural deep water ports, and the strategic importance of its location, both militarily and commercially, propelled Key West to the forefront of prominence nationally. This then is our community, and this is the story of our parish.

The story begins in the New World, where Florida is a blank page waiting to be written on by Catholic explorers and clergy. Now, turn the pages and follow the path of Catholicism as its seeds were introduced into our land, took root in Key West, and were nurtured in our parish to gain the honor of a Minor Basilica.

*Bobby Bernreuter*

**(PD art)**

# Chapter 1
## The Discovery Missions

Now I will set the stage so that the reader may grasp the untamed vastness of 16th century Florida. Large swamps of sawgrass and islands lacking sustainable fresh water predominated the south. The interior was lush with pines, palmettos, and hardwoods. In the center was a huge lake known by the natives as *Mayaimi,* meaning Big Water. The land was hot, humid, had fierce storms, and even fiercer mosquitoes. It was inhabited by bears, cougars, alligators, poisonous snakes, and an estimated 350,000 indigenous people.

(PD art)

These native people were generally well over six feet tall, well proportioned, and attractive. They lived into their eighties. Comparatively the average Spaniard of that time would be four feet, nine inches and live about fifty years. Because of the warm climate, the natives wore little more than a loin cloth which covered what modesty required. They possessed handsome cloaks made with all types of animal skins which were worn for warmth or ceremonies. Their hair was worn long and caught up in a large knot on top of the head. This would be adorned with threads of color and tall feathers the number and height of which would distinguish the caciques and princes of their people.

(PD art)

They lived in large cities with up to 600 houses or small villages with fewer than 200 houses. The houses of the caciques (the great chief or king) would be large enough to hold 500 to 1,000 people and would be divided into many rooms for their family and nobility, with a major hall in the middle. Often these caciques' houses were placed on man-made hills up to fourteen feet in height.

All the men carried bows and arrows as their principal means of defense and hunting. Trained with it since childhood they were very adept in its use. The bow was of the same height of the man who carried it. Made of oak or other hardwoods and extremely powerful, the typical Spaniard could not draw it past his face, whereas the Indian could easily draw it past his ear.

This was a noble race, a proud people skilled in battle from constant warring between their nations. They showed no fear of death and abhorred disgrace, dishonor, and cowardice. They would either make slaves of their enemies or torture and kill them; yet they proved to be generous and honorable to their allies. They believed in a higher spiritual power that was manifested in the sun and the moon, but did not build tributes or perform ceremonies to honor them. They did honor their deceased kings and nobility by keeping their bones in large temples which they constructed for that purpose.

This then is the theatre the religious had to work in, and the brutality of the early explorers is partially to blame for the animosity they encountered from the natives. This is also our beginning, the larger world from which our island was first cultivated.

**1513**     Our history begins on March 3, in the year 1513. On this day the great Spanish explorer, Ponce de Leon and about two hundred men sailed from Puerto Rico on three ships outfitted at his own expense: the *Santa Maria*, the *Santiago*, and the *San Cristobal*. He was in search of a fabled land called "Bimini", where, according to the local natives, this island was brimming with gold and contained a precious fountain whose waters preserved the youth of all who drank from it.

**Ponce de Leon** (PD art)

The search for this miraculous water took his small fleet through the Bahamas with no success. Not to be denied his adventure, he continued sailing towards the northwest, where the natives had convinced him a great land existed. Finally, on Easter Sunday of March 27, 1513, Ponce de Leon sighted this new land. With his small entourage, he continued to sail northward along the coast, searching for a safe harbor or anchorage. On April 2, 1513, somewhere in the vicinity of St. Augustine, they found such a place and put ashore.

Since it was the custom of early Spanish explorers to bestow on new lands the name of the Catholic feast day on which it was discovered, he called this land "La Florida", as this was the Easter Season known in Spain as "Pascua Florida" (meaning Flowery Passover) and claimed it for the Spanish Crown.

Although future explorations would include Catholic clergy, this voyage did not, so they were unable to celebrate their arrival with the customary Mass. Continuing his exploration of this territory to the south, he passed by a chain of islands which the Spanish historian Antonio de Herrera describes in his

acclaimed work, *Historia general de los hechos de los Castellanos en las islas y tierra firme del Mar Oceano*:

**"On Sunday, the Feast of the Holy Spirit, the 15th of May (1513) they ran along the coast of rocky islets ten leagues, as far as the two white rocky inlets. To all this line of islands and rocky islets they gave the name of 'Los Martires' because seen from a distance the rocks, as they rose to view, appeared like men who were suffering; and the name remained fitting, because of the many that have been lost there since."**

Today these islands are called the Florida Keys. Sailing around the southern end of this chain of islands, Ponce de Leon continued his journey westward and finally encountered an island with many sea turtles. In need of water and provisions, he sent a party ashore, but failing to find any, this island was given the descriptive name, the "Dry Tortugas". After exploring along the Gulf Coast of La Florida, perhaps as far north as Port Charlotte, he returned to Puerto Rico.

Ponce de Leon's discovery of this new land pleased the King of Spain, Ferdinand II, enough to bestow upon him the title of 'Adelantado de La Florida' or 'Governor of Florida'. Along with the title came the authority to conquer, convert, and colonize this new territory. Thus began the early missionary years of Florida as a Spanish Territory, for as soon as Ponce de Leon claimed Florida for the Spanish king, it began its spiritual journey into Catholicism. By the time Ponce de Leon returned on his second voyage, Florida would be under the auspices of the Diocese of Baracoa, Cuba. This diocese, erected in 1518, under Bishop Juan de Witte Hoos (Ubite), O.P., encompassed all of Cuba and Florida. (As explorations had not yet determined the extent of this new land, "Florida" was understood to include all territories that future expeditions would conquer.)

Every future exploration carried with it the good intention of spreading Christianity. Henceforth, every explorer would have a contingency of priests who would accompany them throughout the new lands insuring for their men the continued practice of their faith and seeking the conversion of the natives.

**1521**   Ponce de Leon's second visit in 1521 gives us the first documented presence of Catholic priests on the mainland of North America. They would have passed by the Florida Keys where from the decks of his two ships our blessed island would have first fallen under the watchful gaze of Catholic priests.

However, when Ponce de Leon landed on the Gulf Coast around Port Charlotte, he was not treated as well by the Indians as on his first trip. His group had barely disembarked when they were violently attacked by the local natives. In this battle Ponce de Leon was wounded by an arrow and every man

with him, save six, was slain.  It is widely thought that Spanish slave ships may have accosted the Indian towns along the Gulf coast in between de Leon's two voyages which would account for their hostility.  His men hastily returned him to Cuba, where in a few days the old knight and all who were wounded perished.

**1522**       In 1522 the name, Diocese of Baracoa, was changed to the Diocese of Santiago de Cuba.  Florida would remain under that diocese until 1787.

**1526**       Five years after Ponce de Leon's second voyage, Lucas Vázquez de Ayllón, sailed up the east coast as far as Chesapeake Bay, then turned south.  On October 8, they established the short-lived colony of San Miguel de Gualdape, probably at or near present-day Georgia's Sapelo Sound.  Here Vázquez, two Dominican priests, a friar, and six hundred settlers tried to establish their community, but a lack of food, sickness, and finally native troubles soon extinguished their enthusiasm.  Then, after the death of de Ayllón they packed it in and sailed home.  His colony included the first use of black slaves in the new world. Ayllón's colony was the first European colony in what is now the United States, preceding Jamestown, Virginia by 81 years, and St. Augustine, Florida (the first successful colony) by 39 years.

**Lucas Vázquez de Ayllón** (PD art)

**1528**       In April of that year, Panfilo de Narvaez landed just north of Tampa Bay to seek his fortune in the wilderness of Florida.  Although not immediately attacked by the natives, those on shore indicated by signs that he must go back to his ships and sail away.  Not dismayed by their hostility, and entrusted with the duty to convert these savages, he pressed on with his 300 man force.  His deeper conviction however, was to acquire fame and fortune for himself and he challenged the natives to either be baptized or suffer the ravages of war.  He was the most ruthless and incompetent of the early explorers.

In the end, after the loss of many lives, there was no gold, some notoriety, but very little change in the faith of the Indians.  He fled Florida with what was left of his men from the shores of Pensacola in five hurriedly built boats.  Four were lost at sea, including Narvaez.  Only one boat survived with four men.  Eight years later these four would reach Mexico by foot.

**(PD art)**
**Panfilo de Narvaez**

Although most of the encounters with the natives ended poorly, as severe cruelties were practiced by both sides, there was one story of compassion that deserves note.

Juan Ortiz was a young soldier serving under de Narvaez; he was captured by the tribal chief Hirrihigua. Previously, Hirrihigua had been tortured brutally by the Spaniards in an attempt to have him disclose where their gold was hidden. Thus in retaliation he would frequently torture this young man, Juan Ortiz.

On one occasion Ortiz was placed on a smoking rack and faced a certain death. The chief's daughter pleaded for his life and Hirrihigua relented, but later would attempt to kill him again. This young Indian maiden then helped him escape to another tribe where she was betrothed to the chief. The chief took Ortiz in and protected him until the arrival of de Soto ten years later.

**1539**    Hernando de Soto, newly commissioned as Adelantado of Florida and of Cuba, arrived in 1539 with nine ships, 620 men (12 clergy), and 220 horses, in what is now known as Shaw's Point in Bradenton, Florida. He named the bay "Espiritu Santo" (Holy Spirit) as it was Whitsunday (the feast of Pentecost) when he arrived. This was just south of where the explorer, Panfilo de Narvaez had landed ten years before. Narvaez's mission to discover gold had failed miserably at the hands of the local natives and now de Soto was undertaking a similar enterprise and ultimately would face a similar demise.

**Hernando de Soto**
(PD art)

For his part de Soto sought peace with the Indians. However, there were many battles with those who resisted his expedition. By necessity, he would take many prisoners to act as guides, interpreters, and domestics. At times he would decimate the fields and villages of hostile nations to punish them and insure their submission to facilitate his quest for gold. In spite of their smaller stature, the skills of his cavaliers on horseback, for the most part, gave the Spaniards a decided advantage on open ground. He was often described by the natives as a "sun god" and some believed him immortal.

Let me relate the story of the most dreadful of de Soto's military encounters with the Indians. It was the battle of Mauvila (Mabila) where his expedition was deceived into thinking that this nation was friendly when it was always their intention to trap and kill all the Spaniards. The Indians turned their entire village over to de Soto and his troops to lure them inside the walls. Once trapped inside the Indians set fire to their own homes to kill the Spanish within.

According to Garcilaso, it was a terrible battle lasting throughout the night, with the Spanish caught so off guard as not to have had time to armor themselves or mount their horses; they were forced to fight in their nightshirts, without pants or boots. Their only light was from the fires of the houses they had fled from.

Because of their superb military experience and discipline the Spanish proved victorious and suffered the loss of only 82 soldiers and 45 horses. The Indians' loss amounted to probably over five thousand, virtually the entire village. As horrendous as this sounds, all this loss of life was not deemed the greatest of their losses. The following text is taken from *The Florida of the Inca*, by Garcilaso de la Vega, pg. 382.

**The loss of the Spaniards was even more serious than that of the destruction of their companions and horses whom the Indians had killed; for there were other things which they esteemed even more when they considered the purpose for which they had been dedicated, such, for instance, as a small quantity of wheat flour (three bushels in all) and sixteen gallons of wine. This was all they possessed of these materials when they arrived in Mauvila, and for many days back they had guarded and preserved them for the Masses to be said in their behalf. In order that they might travel in better care and greater safety, the Governor himself had brought them with his equipage. But all were burned along with the chalices, altars and sacerdotal vestments carried for divine worship. Hence, from that place on, it was not possible to hear Mass, for they had no bread and wine for the consecration of the Eucharist. And although among the priests, the religious and the seculars there were disputes in theology as to whether or not they would be able to consecrate bread made from corn, it was agreed by common consent that the most certain thing that the Holy Roman Church, Our Mother and Lady, commands and teaches each of us in her sacred decrees and canons is that this bread must be of wheat and the wine of grapes. Thus these Catholic Spaniards made no efforts to find dubious substitutes because they held no doubt in regard to their obedience to their Mother, the Roman Catholic Church; and they also desisted because even had they possessed materials for the consecration of the Eucharist, they still lacked the chalices and altars for its celebration.**

An ocean away from home: continuously fighting Indians, hunger, and disease; daily marching through mosquito infested marshes and thick humid forests; these devout men treasured the Sacrament of the Eucharist more than life. Their reverence should give us pause to reflect on our own devoutness to the Blessed Sacrament and the Holy Mass.

Three years after starting his explorations of the southeast, de Soto died of a semitropical fever in the native village of Guachoya, on the western banks of the Mississippi. To prevent the Indians from learning of his mortality, his body was weighed down and cast into the Mississippi River at night. Of the 620 soldiers who initially accompanied him, less than half survived by making their way to Mexico in hastily made boats.

**1549**    While no attempts were made to explore the Florida Keys during this period, the unfortunate combination of storms and reefs insured the occasional presence of shipwrecked survivors to the islands. Of note was thirteen year old Hernando de Escalante Fontaneda, who was shipwrecked and captured by the Calusa Indians of the upper keys. He lived with them for 17 years until his rescue in 1566.

His memoirs recall the tribes, villages, and conduct of the Native Americans. He writes:

There are yet other islands, nearer to the mainland, stretching between the west and east, called the Martires; for the reason that many men have suffered on them, and also because certain rocks rise there from beneath the sea, which, at a distance, look like men in distress.

"Indians are on these islands, who are of a large size: the women are well proportioned, and have good countenances. On these islands there are two Indian towns; in one of them the one town is called Guarugunbe, which in Spanish is pueblo de Llanto, the town of weeping; the name of the other little town, Cuchiyaga, means the place where there has been suffering...

...Toward the north the Martires end near a place the Indians called Tequesta, situated on the bank of a river which extends into the country the distance of fifteen leagues, and issues from another lake of fresh water, which is said by some Indians who have traversed it more than I, to be an arm of the Lake of Mayaimi...

...The Jordan that is talked of, is a superstition of the Indians of Cuba, which they hold to because it is their creed, not because there is such a river. Juan Ponz de Leon, giving heed to the tale of the Indians of Cuba and Santo Domingo, went to Florida in search of the River Jordan, that he might have some enterprise on foot, or that he might earn greater fame than he already possessed and close his life, which is the most probable supposition; or, if not for these objects, then that he might become young from bathing in such a stream. This thought was of itself proof that all must have been fiction that was told by the Indians of Cuba and its whole neighborhood, who, to satisfy their tradition, said that the Jordan was in Florida; to which at least I can say, that while I was a captive there, I bathed in many streams, but to my misfortune I never came upon the river. (NOTE: Cuchiyaga was the Indian name for Key West.)

And indeed, King Carlos, the great Cacique of the Calusas, enabled Hernando to travel throughout most of South Florida giving us a unique perspective of the great Spanish exploitations of the territory. The tribes continuously fought amongst themselves and would indenture those captives that were not tortured and killed. The same fate awaited any shipwreck victim unlucky enough to fall into their hands.

That Florida would not be tamed easily became apparent, as the natives proved more formidable and resourceful than the Spanish soldiers anticipated. Explorers and investors were now reluctant to finance an expedition with such low odds of success. But not all treasures are of the earthly kind. There are treasures to be stored in heaven and this history would be remiss not to include the endeavors of Father Luis Cancer de Barbastro, a Dominican priest.

After reading the reports of the earlier explorers to La Florida, Father Barbastro concluded that it was their militant approach that angered the natives and turned them against the Spaniards. He petitioned his order and the Spanish government to allow him to try a pacifist approach that was used with much success in La Verapaz territory of Guatemala.

In a letter Fray Luis wrote to Las Casas and an official of the Council of the Indies, he stated, **"...four tyrants had gone to Florida who, instead of accomplishing any good, had done so much harm, [that it was] thought advisable to assign its pacific conquest to friars and to give them assistance in their undertaking."**

In 1549 his request was granted and the vessel, *Santa Maria de la Encina,* was outfitted and put at his disposal without the accustomed military escort. Three other Dominican priests accompanied him: Fathers Gregorio de Beteta, Diego de Tolosa, and Juan Garcia. A Spanish oblate named Fuentes also joined the daring band. A royal decree was issued which required all Indian slaves be returned with this voyage to show good will and hopefully further enhance the success of the mission. Among them, an Indian woman named Magdalena was to be their interpreter.

The idea was to land somewhere that had not been previously visited and thereby corrupted by military encounters. However, the captain put them ashore near Espritu Santo Bay, where de Soto had landed. Appearing friendly at first, the Indians quickly sized up these new visitors. They became more and more demanding, and somehow unnoticed, they separated Magdalena, Fr. Diego de Tolosa, and the oblate brother Fuentes from the others. When Fr. Cancer asked about their whereabouts, he was told that they had gone to see the tribal chief and would be brought back soon.

Fr. Cancer returned the next day with more presents to appease the natives, but they seemed to have vanished. The expedition then sailed up the coast for a little over a week searching for their lost comrades until they found a harbor which the Indians had spoken of. Fr. Cancer went ashore but the place seemed deserted, then just as he was about to return to the ship he heard cries in broken Spanish, "Amigo, amigo... bueno, bueno!" A group of Indians materialized out of the forest with Magdalena, his Indian interpreter, who having discarded her Christian clothing, had now joined with the natives. She convinced Fr. Cancer that a chief with many Indians were gathered nearby and were waiting to hear his preaching.

Excited he returned to his ship to plan the next day's mission to these natives. However once on board the vessel, his enthusiasm was quelled by the presence of Juan Muñoz, one of de Soto's soldiers who had been enslaved by the Indians ten years earlier and just made his escape. He informed the good priest that Father Diego and the lay brother had both been murdered by the natives and the sailor who had taken them ashore was now held in bondage.

Not dismayed, Fr. Cancer resolved to reach out to these people with charity and forgiveness. After several days waiting for calmer seas, Fr. Cancer, Fr. Gregorio, and the escaped soldier, Juan Muñoz, along with a small crew, were rowed toward the beach. The sight of many Indians aggressively displaying clubs, bows, and darts alarmed the expedition causing Fr. Gregorio to warn his companion not to go ashore. Undaunted, Fr. Cancer leapt out of the boat and waded to the beach. He approached the Indians and fell to his knees in prayer. He was quickly surrounded by the natives, who removed his Dominican hat and quickly dispatched him with a vicious swipe of a club. The others quickly returned to the ship and, disheartened, sailed away.

**1559**     That is the year Don Tristan de Luna made a last, futile attempt to convert the Indians. He landed near the future site of Pensacola with 1,500 soldiers, settlers and priests and a year's worth of provisions. With much disappointment he returned to Mexico and King Phillip II declared that Spain would make no further attempts to settle Florida.

**1562**     Florida, because of its proximity to the Bahama Channel (Straits of Florida) and easy access to the passing treasure fleets of Spain, would remain too tempting a prize to ignore for long. And so the French explorer Jean Ribault, with the blessings of twelve year old King Charles IX, landed his two ships in the harbor of Port Royal. There he built Fort Caroline to protect his small settlement of French Huguenots (Protestants) and conduct raids on Spanish ships.

This French fort was established near the mouth of the St. John's River, the same land claimed by Spain.

**Jean Ribault**     (PD art)

**1565**     King Phillip II was quick to change his mind upon learning of Ribault's audacity to build a fort on Spanish territory. He commissioned Pedro Menéndez de Avilés, Captain General of the Indies Fleet to engage these French interlopers, destroy their fort, and establish once and for all a permanent Spanish community in Florida.

Menéndez saw this as an opportunity to search for his son who was reportedly lost somewhere on the Florida coast. Appointed Adelantado, he was to secure both the Bahama Channel and the spirituality of the Florida natives from these heretical Huguenots.

Captain General Menéndez and his crew sighted the coast of La Florida on the Feast of Saint Augustine, August 28, 1565. They landed on September 8, the Feast of the Nativity of the Blessed Virgin Mary, at a site they named "Nombre de Dios". Menéndez knelt and kissed a wooden cross presented to him by his chaplain, Father Francisco López de Mendoza Grajales, and then celebrated the first Mass.

Menéndez established this settlement in the former Timucua village of Seloy, naming it St. Augustine, in honor of that saints feast day, the day he first sighted this new land. This would become the first parish, in the first permanent European settlement, in what would later be a part of the United States of America.

Three days later Menéndez wrote to King Phillip II,

*As for myself, Your Majesty may be assured that if I had a million (ducats) more or less, I would spend it all upon this undertaking, because it is of such great service to God Our Lord, for the increase of our Holy Catholic Faith, and for the service of Your Majesty, and therefore, I have offered to Our Lord all that He may give me in this world, all that I may acquire and possess, in order to plant the Gospel in this land for the enlightenment of its natives; and in like manner I pledge myself to Your Majesty.*

(PD art)
**Menéndez de Avilés**

There was also a military aspect to the "asiento" or royal contract given to Menéndez and within two weeks he marched overland with five hundred soldiers and captured Fort Caroline. Only women, children, and youths not under arms were spared. Later he captured Jean Ribault and his shipwrecked soldiers just south of St. Augustine. Since the prisoners far outnumbered their captors, they were all executed by sword except the Catholics and youths not under arms.

These were practical military decisions, not unlike those of the English, French, and other expeditionary forces of this era. While we would judge these acts as barbaric, similar atrocities occur in our modern age of warfare.

With the approval of Bishop Juan del Castillo, of the Diocese of Santiago de Cuba, Menéndez appointed Fr. Grajales as the first parish priest of St. Augustine. Lacking sufficient numbers of priests, Menéndez directed qualified soldiers to give religious instructions to the Indians while he awaited the arrival of Jesuit missionaries. He set out to accomplish by conversion what the other explorers had failed to do with threats.

Do not be misled into thinking that times had changed and conversions were easy for Menéndez; that is far from reality. Not only did he have to contend with a shortage of clergy, but disease, starvation, and the distrust of many Indian chiefs.

[**Author's note**: The original 600 Catholic soldiers and colonists of St. Augustine would have been dead or very old, when forty-two years later, John Smith and his small group of English settlers landed at Jamestown in 1607, forming the first English settlement. And by the time the Pilgrims landed on Plymouth Rock in 1620, the city of St. Augustine was already 55 years old.]

**1566**     In June a relief expedition arrived with five diocesan priests. They were placed under Fr. López's authority, who now referred to himself as the "Vicar of Florida". Then in September of that year, three Jesuits arrived in answer to Menéndez's petitions: Father Pedro Martínez, superior, Father Juan Rogel, and Brother Francisco Villareal. They were sent by St. Francis Borgia, the founder of Jesuit missions in Florida.

Unfortunately they missed the harbor of St. Augustine and landed near the mouth of the St. John's River. Fr. Martínez and eight crew rowed ashore to seek directions; while ashore a storm arose and pushed their ship out to sea leaving them stranded. Two weeks later, surviving with the help of friendly natives, Father Martínez and crew were attacked and all but four killed by warring Indians. Father Martínez was strangled underwater and clubbed to death while holding his crucifix to his breast. Thus the first Jesuit to set foot in Florida was martyred.

**1567**     The ship, tossed by the storm, made its way to Havana where Menéndez's rescue ships found them. Early in 1567 they were brought back to Florida. Father Juan Rogel, from Havana was sent near present day Charlotte Harbor to convert the Calusa Indians while Brother Francisco Villareal came down to Biscayne Bay to minister to the Tequesta.

This mission to Biscayne Bay, near the present city of Miami, was significant because of its proximity to Cuba. Menéndez established the outpost himself, staying there for four days and planting a cross, thereby introducing Catholicism to South Florida.

Also this year a Spanish mission was reportedly established on Upper Matecumbe Key to minister to the Los Cayos natives. These Native Americans were soon decimated by smallpox and measles, which brought that mission to an end.

**1572**     By 1572 the Jesuit authorities in Spain decided to abandon altogether the mission field of Florida and the few remaining missionaries were recalled to Mexico. As soon as the Jesuits left, Menéndez requested the Franciscan Fathers, the Friars Minor, to take up the cross of converting his Florida natives.

This same year Menéndez was recalled to Spain to direct an "invincible armada" to clear the Flanders coast of pirates. St. Augustine had cost him his health and his wealth, neither of which he considered of any serious consequence. On September 8, 1574, in a letter to his nephew in Florida, he writes,

*"After the salvation of my soul, there is nothing I desire more than to be in Florida, to end my days saving souls..."* Nine days later he died.

**1573**     The first Franciscans arrived in Florida; they would never exceed more than four or five their first years here. But in 1578 they began a concerted effort to convert the native population and in the ensuing 100 years they would attain more than thirty successful missions and 26,000 conversions.

**1586**     Sir Francis Drake, an English Captain, sighted St. Augustine while returning from the West Indies. His crew landed and burned the Spanish settlement to the ground. St. Augustine was rebuilt slowly, as Spain had more interest in the conversion of the Indians than the welfare of the small colony of settlers.

**1593**     Twelve missionaries of the order of St. Francis came and ministered to several native villages on the coast not far from St. Augustine. They were successful in their teachings and converted a great number of the Indians.

**1595**     Franciscan superior Fray Francisco Marrón, arrived in St. Augustine with a new group of missionaries. They remained for many years. The friars were escorted out to the missions personally by the governor, and in view of the natives he knelt and kissed their hands as a sign of the sacred authority granted to them by God.

Although the Franciscans continued with their northern missions, the Jesuits would not return again to Florida until 1743. And so it was, for 198 uninterrupted years: diocesan, then Jesuit, and finally Franciscan missionaries, would carry Christianity and civilization into the Florida wilderness.

These missionaries were a critical force in the colonization of the New World. They were emissaries not only for Christ, but for commerce, the military, and the Spanish government, serving multiple purposes by befriending and converting the Native American tribes. By their ardent labors these missionaries and explorers laid down the roots of our Catholic heritage in Florida.

The Crown of Spain, by virtue of the "Patronato Real de Indias" or Royal Patronage of the Indies, granted by Pope Julius II in 1508, had complete ecclesiastical authority over Florida. This was an era when the government and the church worked in unity. The king was for all practical purposes the vicar of the Pope. He directed the missionaries, paid them, built their churches and friaries. He exercised the same authority over the secular priests and their parishes. He also provided for the health, welfare, and conversion of the natives with no expectation of financial return on the investments. His only consideration was for the vast numbers of souls now directed toward heaven.

(PD art)
**King Phillip II of Spain**

# Chapter 2
## The Early Missions

**1600**   The seventeenth century would see the rise and fall of the Franciscan missions in Florida with most of their efforts expended in the northern half of the state and in what is now Georgia. Since the founding of St. Augustine, because of the distance and dangers involved, only two of the twenty-three Cuban prelates had ever visited the territory. Because of this and growing tensions between the Franciscan missionaries and the bishops of Cuba, two of the Florida governors, Rebolledo in 1655 and Cabrera in 1683, had requested that Florida be separated from the diocese of Santiago de Cuba. In fact there were similar sentiments in Cuba that Florida should be ecclesiastically and financially separated from Havana, but this would not happen for another 100 years.

During this period there are few records to be found concerning Key West or the Florida Keys. However we know that Cuban fisherman working in the waters surrounding the Keys and Key West were able to secure the natives' friendship with tokens of trinkets, colored cloth, and rum.

**1622**   Wrecks continued to occur frequently on the reefs and by the time the great hurricane of 1622 destroyed the Spanish treasure fleet, sinking the *Atocha, Santa Margarita*, and *Nuestra Señora del Rosario*, the natives, with more than 100 years of experience, had become very adept at diving and salvaging. Because of these skills, they were employed by the Spanish to recover the silver and gold.

**1690**   Cayo Hueso became well known in Cuban markets as trading with the natives, along with the fishing industry, had become commonplace. Not waiting on the Spanish trading vessels, many of the Keys' natives began plying their wares in Havana, making the daring crossing of the Florida Straits in their dugout canoes. They realized that being Catholic made them more acceptable when trading with the Spaniards so they sought out Cuban priests to baptize them. However once back in the Keys, without any religious support, they would return to their pagan lifestyle.

**1700**   Over these last hundred years there were wars between the French, the English, and the Indians. More European colonies had been formed and a large percentage of the Indians succumbed to the newly introduced diseases. Those Indians that survived had adopted the Spanish culture and language. Some even began fishing cooperatively with the Spanish and industry flourished between the two groups.

**1709**   This year was distinguished by the arrival of Florida's first resident bishop. Still under the auspices of Santiago de Cuba, Auxiliary Bishop Dionisio Resino, the oldest priest in Cuba, was assigned the position. Discouraged by the lack of parish buildings and the loss of converts, Bishop Resino returned to Cuba three weeks after arriving. It would be more than twenty years before his replacement arrived.

**1711**   Upon learning that British backed Indians from North Florida, most likely tribes of the Creek Confederacy, were raiding the tribes of South Florida, destroying the missions, and selling the Indians as slaves, Bishop Jerónimo Nosti de Valdés, O.S.Bas. in Cuba, sent Captain Luis Perdomo with two ships to rescue the Keys' Indians. However due to lack of space on the ships, he was only able to rescue 270 of the natives. Of those, all but 70 died of diseases in Cuba and eventually 18 returned to Florida.

**1722**   Most early encounters with the Keys' Indians did not end well for the Europeans; therefore, there are few written accounts. However, Father Pierre F.X. de Charlevoix was aboard the French ship *Adour*, bound for Santo Domingo from Biloxi, when she struck a reef off the Florida Keys. The priest recorded his adventures in a journal which was later published.

Upon encountering the Indians he found that they could speak some Spanish and claimed to have been baptized in Havana. Assuring their Indian leader, Don Antonio, that the French were allies of the Spanish, he was able to secure their assistance. He later met their King, Don Diego. Unlike the other Indians, Diego was very short. Diego explained that he was a minor king and therefore under the authority of a much greater king, probably the Cacique of the Calusa.

**1724**   The first European settlers on Key West were mostly migratory fisherman from Cuba, who would fish the clear bountiful waters surrounding the island. They would keep their catch alive by placing them in large holding pens they had constructed in the harbor until they were ready to bring them to the Havana market.

Because of this small settlement of Cubans and Indians there are indications that a parish, staffed by a Cuban priest, might have been established in Key West as early as 1724. Certainly during this period, whether a parish or not, the Holy Mass was celebrated on our island. However, the unpredictable nature of the Keys' natives and the lack of government protection against the English raiders from the Carolinas, forced the missionaries to return to Cuba in 1727. After that, records show that a priest was only able to visit Key West once or twice a year.

**1735**     Newly consecrated, Bishop Francisco de San Buenaventura arrived in St. Augustine from Vera Cruz. As the new auxiliary bishop of Florida, he found himself in the midst of spiritual decadence, scandals, and drunken Indians, plus English traders preaching heretical doctrines on the streets. It took him five years to bring the city back to its Christian values. He was then transferred to the See of Yucatán in 1745.

**1743**     In 1743, two Italian Jesuit priest-explorers, Fathers Joseph Alana and Joseph Monaco, arrived in Cayo Hueso from Havana and opened a mission chapel for Native Americans. These missionaries arduously labored for God. There was no physical reward except disease, heat, and mosquitoes. There was no glory or fame as they are hardly remembered. Their lives were constantly at risk with the natives. They didn't aspire to ascend in rank and most likely they would die of a tropical illness. But they persevered and continued to work their way up the Keys and eventually built another chapel at Biscayne Bay, near what is now Miami.

So what was their motivation? It was love and fear. Their overwhelming love for God: to please Him by bringing more souls to His Kingdom. And fear, a fear that these people would never experience the joys of heaven. You must remember, this was pre-Vatican II, and it was commonly believed that an unbaptized soul could not enter the Kingdom. Their perils and discomfort notwithstanding, they labored in the vineyard because they believed. They remained until the Spanish governor, still unable to offer them protection, ordered them back to Cuba.

**1754**     Nine years after his appointment as auxiliary bishop of Florida, Father Pedro Ponce y Carrasco, of Cuba, finally visits the territory. However, not healthy enough to fulfill his commission, he returned to Cuba a mere ten months later.

### The French and Indian War 1755-1763

**1755**     During the French and Indian War (Seven Years War) Spain joined with France to fight the English. The war did not go well for Spain and her ally France, and both lost territory to the British. England, now in possession of all the land east of the Mississippi, except for the territory known as New Orleans, desperately wanted to add Florida to its possessions. After capturing Cuba in 1762, a prize possession which Spain was anxious to get back, Britain easily arranged a trade for Florida which was spelled out in the First Treaty of Paris. You must realize that Cuba had been domesticated and cultivated by Spain for over 250 years and was strategically much more important to the Spanish national interest than the two Florida cities of St. Augustine and Pensacola.

## British Occupation

**1763**     This year began the Spanish withdrawal and the British occupation of Florida, which brought most of the missions to an end. Despite the fact that the treaty provided that the Spanish who remained in Florida would be allowed to practice their Catholic faith and maintain property rights, almost all left on ships which were provided to remove them to Cuba or Mexico where the Spanish King Charles III, offered them free homes to relocate. The European population of Florida primarily existed in only two cities: St. Augustine and Pensacola.

Having not been treated well in the past by the British, many of what remained of our local Native Americans fled with the Spanish. At this time about eighty families of Calusa natives had reportedly taken refuge from the British by fleeing to Key West and Key Vaca, and they also were taken to Cuba.

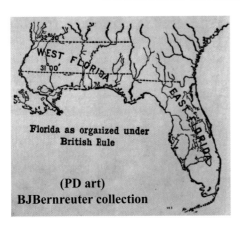

Florida as organized under British Rule

(PD art)
BJBernreuter collection

The British divided Florida into two parts: East Florida, with its capital at St. Augustine; and West Florida, with Pensacola as its capital. During the next twenty years of the Protestant British occupation of Florida, there was no recorded activity by the Catholic Church; it is believed that only eight Catholics remained in the entire state. Along with British rule came British colonialism. The English were offering land and farming incentives to attract settlers to this new territory and if they had been able to keep possession of Florida for more than twenty years it might have paid off.

I seriously doubt that any of this was of particular concern to the transient settlement in Cayo Hueso because of their close ties to Cuba and the lack of any English jurisdiction on the island. In fact, Spain claimed that the Florida Keys were a part of Cuba and therefore not included in the land trade with England. They even referred to the Keys as "Norte de Havana" and continued issuing fishing licenses for the Keys. Now, with the threat of the natives gone, the Bahamians were coming over in greater numbers and establishing camps to take advantage of the Keys' resources: hunting turtles, cutting the valuable mahogany trees, and salvaging wrecks.

**1767**     A faction of the Creek Indians and other Muskogean speaking natives joined together and immigrated into the territory from the North. They then became known as "Seminoles", which in their language means "runaway" because they had left their tribal lands in Georgia and Alabama and settled in Florida. They also absorbed the few remnants of the aboriginal natives left in Florida. In later years they would directly impact the citizens of the Keys.

## American Revolution

**1776**     When the American Colonies declared their independence from England in 1776, Florida and the Bahamas were still Royal Colonies and offered refuge to many southern Loyalists (Tories) fleeing from Georgia and the Carolinas. As for Key West, it would have had little meaning. The winter mullet run would have been of more interest to these hardy souls than what was happening to some British colonies more than a thousand miles to the north. Key West of the eighteenth century was a far cry from the cares and woes of northern Florida.

Flag of 1876 by BJBernreuter

**1779**     Spain did not officially recognize the U.S. but became an informal ally when it declared war on Britain on June 21, 1779. Bernardo de Gálvez y Madrid, governor of Louisiana and general of the Spanish forces in New Spain, led a surprise invasion of West Florida against the British and kept open a vital conduit for supplies to the Americans. In 1782, after the British defeat at Yorktown, a Spanish fleet appeared off the coast of Nassau, and the British surrendered the Bahamas without a fight.

## Florida a Spanish Territory

**1783**     Global hostilities between the American Colonies, Britain, France, and Spain, ended in 1783, with the signing of peace treaties in Versailles, (also known as the Treaty of Paris). Through this document, England ceded East and West Florida back to Spain in exchange for the Bahama Islands.

The fact that Spain would trade Florida, a territory about twice the size it is today, to ransom Havana in 1763, and then for England to trade off this same territory to regain the Bahamas twenty years later, speaks to the expense and difficulty in cultivating and governing this wilderness frontier.

While a few English remained, most were taken aboard ships to Nova Scotia, the Bahamas, or returned to England in a reversal of the events twenty years earlier. By 1788, about 9,300 Tories had fled to the Bahamas and more would follow, but their American experience would later entice them to return.

**1787**     During this exodus of the British it seems very few of the previous Spanish residents returned from Cuba. By 1787, the West Florida capital of Pensacola was left with a population of only 265. In the East Florida province only 900 Caucasian and 490 black slaves made up the entire population. Of these, more than two hundred were Anglo-Americans living in the northern frontier.

King Charles III dispensed with the Spanish law requiring all English residents to convert to Catholicism and instead directed that they should be won over by "gentle preaching". He further decreed that special parishes should be erected for these English, and that Irish priests must be found, who could speak their language.

It is not surprising that Florida's second Spanish period, from 1783 to 1821, would show little progression as far as the Catholic Church was concerned. The twenty years of Protestant rule combined with the upheaval of relocation, along with the shortage of missionary priests, left the few remnants of Catholicism to survive on their own.

Yet the Catholics of Key West had survived. Living in this close knit island community, the hardy residents were able to sustain the economic dislocation, political disruption, and cultural shock occurring throughout the rest of the territory. Mainly because of their geographic isolation from the mainland, they really were more of a Cuban community, which allowed them to weather these transitional years more easily than the Catholic communities throughout the rest of Florida.

On September 10, 1787, the Holy See in Rome divided the diocese of Santiago, and Florida was transferred to the newly erected diocese of San Cristobal de la Habana, Cuba, which had direct ties to this island village. The new diocese was under the direction of its first Bishop, the Most Rev. Felipe José de Tres-Palacios y Verdeja.

**1793**
In New Orleans, Don Luis Ignacio Penalver y Cardenas of Havana was consecrated Bishop of the new Diocese of Louisiana. This diocese, erected by Pope Pius VI, included both East and West Florida. Although he never visited his province of Florida, Bishop Penalver did have a major impact in the development of the faith here.

In a letter to his pastors he ordered an annual census to be taken, and among things to be specified, was how many Negroes, free and slave, Catholic and non-Catholic, were living within the parochial boundaries. Among other things, owners of slaves were bound to properly feed, clothe, and give them the Christian instruction necessary for the reception of the sacraments.

(PD art)
**Bishop Don Luis Ignacio Penalver**

## War of 1812

**1812**    This historic event is important to our parish's history because if it were not for the peculiarities and outcome of the war our Masses would be primarily in Spanish now rather than English.

During the conflicts leading up to the War of 1812, there was a growing fear that England would try to seize Florida to gain an advantage over the United States. At the same time, seeing an opportunity for his people, the great Shawnee chief Tecumseh inflamed the tribes of the Northwest to rid the American settlers from lands north of the Ohio.

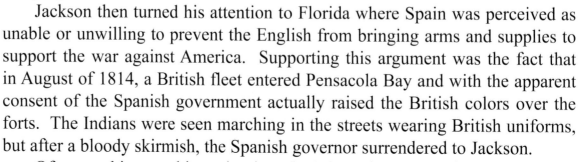
Tecumseh uniting the tribes.
(PD art)
Bergreuter collection

His plans were aided by the British at Pensacola, who encouraged the war and furnished the Indians with arms. This collaboration divided the American military.

In the resulting Creek War, General Andrew Jackson defeated the Red Sticks in Alabama, at the Battle of Horseshoe Bend, in 1814. Both Sam Houston and David Crockett served under Jackson in these campaigns. Crockett would also serve as a scout for Jackson in his Florida campaign.

Jackson then turned his attention to Florida where Spain was perceived as unable or unwilling to prevent the English from bringing arms and supplies to support the war against America. Supporting this argument was the fact that in August of 1814, a British fleet entered Pensacola Bay and with the apparent consent of the Spanish government actually raised the British colors over the forts. The Indians were seen marching in the streets wearing British uniforms, but after a bloody skirmish, the Spanish governor surrendered to Jackson.

Of course his armed intrusion into Spain's territory caused an international incident and Jackson was accused of excessive hostilities. His directions however, were to "terminate the conflict" and Jackson believed the best way to do this was to seize Florida. Before going, Jackson wrote to President Monroe, ***"Let it be signified to me through any channel ... that the possession of the Floridas would be desirable to the United States, and in sixty days it will be accomplished."*** President Monroe had been secretly given congressional approval for the U.S. Military to take Florida by force if it became necessary. Thus he had given Jackson orders that were purposely ambiguous enough to allow international denials if it became necessary.

**1815**    After defeating the British at Pensacola General Jackson went on to win the famous Battle of New Orleans and his place in American history. Many were calling for Jackson to be censured, but the Secretary of State, John Quincy Adams, an early believer in Manifest Destiny, defended Jackson.

(PD art)
**General Andrew Jackson**

Jackson was nicknamed "Old Hickory" because of his toughness and aggressive personality. He even fought in duels, some fatal to his opponents. After his military career, General Jackson became a politician and was subsequently named Florida's first military governor; he served from March 10, 1821, to December 31, 1821. He was later elected the seventh President of the United States (1829–1837). His enthusiastic followers created the modern Democratic Party.

His bold actions incited the U.S. government to pressure Spain into ceding Florida to the United States. But before that would take place, on August 26, 1815, Don Juan de Estrada, the Adelantado of Florida, granted to a young Spanish officer, Juan Pablo Salas, the entire island of Cayo Hueso in payment for his services rendered to the king.

**1819**    In 1819, the United States followed through with its intentions of acquiring Florida. By demanding reparation for war debts, assessed at five million dollars, and citing the inability of Spain to properly govern its settlements, the United States annexed the territory of Florida by the Adams–Onís Treaty. Ratifications to this effect were officially exchanged in Washington D.C. on February 22, 1821. Key West was now a part of this new nation, the United States of America.

Flag of 1819
by BJBernreuter

Now a territory of the United States, new settlers arrived in Key West. Many of them were from New England, seagoing men with their families, coming to fish and compete with the Bahamian wreckers. Wrecking was soon to become a prosperous business in the Florida Keys. Paralleling this development of society on the island was an increased desire for religious expression; one woman would form the core group of the Catholics on the Island, Ellen Mallory, the first white female settler.

# Chapter 3
## Seeds of Catholicism

**1820**   It was in 1820, that Charles Mallory, an Episcopalian, and his Catholic wife, Ellen, settled in Key West, and soon after, a small Catholic community formed around their family. Charles died shortly after their arrival and Ellen opened a boarding house, the Cocoanut Grove, which became the center of social life and hospitality in Key West. There she nursed many of the sick during numerous outbreaks of Yellow Fever. Ellen, a leading figure in the community, raised her son, Stephen Russell Mallory, in the Catholic faith.

Young Stephen was educated at Spring Hill College and served later as a U.S. Senator from Florida, 1850-1861, and then during the Civil War, as Secretary of the Navy in the Confederacy. He was one of the more prominent Catholic laymen in the U.S. at that time. His name is memorialized in a public square near the pier at the northwest end of the island, "Mallory Square".

During the last days of the Confederacy, Mallory was arrested and imprisoned at Ft. Lafayette, in New York. During this time he underwent a spiritual transformation which is recorded in his diary. He began and ended each day in prayer, asking for the protection of God, the Blessed Mother, and the angels over his wife and four children. The following is an excerpt taken from a letter written to his son Buddy, then a student at Georgetown College:

*Cling to your religion, my son, as the sheet anchor of life here and to come. Never permit yourself to question its great truths, or mysteries. Faith must save you or nothing can; and faith implies mystery. The rationalist who believes only what he can understand… has led away ardent minds of youth from the days of the Grecian philosophers… He cannot be a Christian.*

*I frankly say to you – and not without regret and humiliation – that I too long neglected this, and that I did not give you the proper example. Learn by my present feeling… to do your duty.*

*Before I left Richmond, I visited the Confessional, made a clean breast of it to Almighty God, and partook of the Bl. Sacrament at Charlotte and at Atlanta. You have ever had the example of your mother, whose noble, wife – like devotion I owe my confession and Communion, after years of neglect.*

These words remain as relevant for us and our children today as they did for Buddy.

**1822**   President Monroe appointed William P. Duval as the first civilian territorial governor of Florida in 1822. Duval Street, was named after him. Short and

stout of figure, he had a noted wit, and Washington Irving, once his traveling companion, wrote of him as "Ralph Ringwood" retelling many of his adventures. Considered a fine lawyer, Gov. Duval was fluent in both French and Spanish. He governed Florida for twelve years and was respected by both the settlers and the Indians.

January 19, 1822, was an important milestone in defining the future of Key West, for on this date Juan Pablo Salas, who reportedly had never set foot on the island, sold it for the sum of $2,000 to John W. Simonton in Havana, Cuba. Realizing he would not be able to develop the island by himself, Mr. Simonton divided it into four parts; he kept one and sold one to John Warner, the U.S. Consul at Havana, another to John Mountain, a Commercial Agent in Havana, and the last to the partnership of John Whitehead and John W. Fleming, who were business associates of Simonton.

John Simonton had a summer residence in Washington, D.C. and used his influence with Congressmen and administration officials to further the development of Key West. Through these connections he was instrumental in having the military establish a presence on the island.

In 1827, Simonton was able to convince Congress to establish a territorial court in Key West. He organized the Lafayette Salt Company here, but in his last years he moved to New Orleans. He died in Washington, D.C. in May of 1854 at the age of 65 and was survived by his daughter, Florida Simonton. John Simonton is considered the founder of Key West.

In 1822, Lieutenant Matthew C. Perry, commander of the US Schooner *Shark*, arrived to take command of the island. He hoisted the American flag and in a politically savvy move, called it "Thompson's Island", in honor of Smith Thompson, the Secretary of the Navy. The name didn't take well, and so we still remain the island of two names, Cayo Hueso or Key West.

Since Florida was no longer under Spanish rule the Bishop of Havana petitioned the Vatican for severance of all ecclesiastical ties to the territory. While awaiting a decision from Rome, he sent a request to Bishop John England of the newly erected Diocese of Charleston, South Carolina, to "look after" East Florida as he was the closest Bishop.

**Commodore Matthew C. Perry**
(PD art)

Decisions from Rome did not arrive for many years and subsequently Florida became embroiled in jurisdictional disputes as American prelates were unsure of their boundaries and none showed interest in adding Florida to their troubles.

**1823**     "Allenton", is what Commodore David Porter named the island when he arrived the following year as commander of the West Indies fleet and established a naval depot here. Assigned the compelling task of ridding the Caribbean of pirates, he formed the "West Indies Anti-Piracy Squadron", a mixed fleet of ships which included a steamship ferry, barges, sloops-of-war, and even a decoy merchant ship armed with hidden guns, as well as 1,100 men. The ships were referred to as the "Mosquito Fleet" due to the ability of the shallow drafted vessels to maneuver over the reefs in the Keys. He scoured the Caribbean, the Bahamas, and the Gulf of Mexico, and is credited with ridding the West Indies of piracy.

(PD art)
**Commodore David Porter**

Commodore Porter was not popular with the citizens of Key West as he ruled over the island ruthlessly, taking provisions when and where it pleased him, but he did bring security to the settlers on the island.

June 9, 1823, the Sacred Congregation of Propaganda Fide met in Rome and revoked a brief of 1822 that temporarily had created the vicariate of Alabama-Mississippi which included Florida. It was disclosed that in reality Florida had been without a designated bishop since 1793. Earlier that year, 1823, Bishop Louis DuBourg of Louisiana, accepting that Florida was his responsibility and in need of control, also requested Bishop England to "look after" Florida as his vicar-general.

**1825**     Finally on August 26, 1825, Rome erected Florida and Alabama into a vicariate-apostolic with Father Michael Portier of New Orleans, as bishop. He had only three clergy besides himself and only three congregations in the entire vicariate, St. Augustine, Pensacola, and Mobile, Alabama. It was not long before he also asked Bishop England to continue to "look after" Florida.

**1828**     Key West was now in the hands of investors and with the added security of a military presence it obtained a charter from the Florida territorial legislature and officially became a city in 1828. It is the seventh oldest city in Florida, behind St. Augustine 1565, St. Marks 1639, Pensacola 1698, Tallahassee 1786, Tampa 1823, and St. Andrews (Panama City) 1827. During this time most religious services were non-denominational and were held by transient clergymen in the old courthouse in Jackson Square.

**1829**   On May 15, 1829 at the urging of Bishop Michael Portier of Mobile, Alabama, Pope Pius VIII elevated the Vicariate of Florida and Alabama to the dignity of a diocese. The Catholic population of all of Florida at that time was thought to be about 4,000.

Around the year 1830 Bishop Portier established Spring Hill College and Seminary, at the head of which was the Rev. Mathias Loras. Spring Hill College, for a time in the charge of the Eudist Fathers, was released to the Jesuit Fathers in 1846 and has since been managed successfully by them.

This was the same college young Stephen Mallory attended and would play a part later in the life of one of Key West's most dearly beloved priests, Fr. Joseph F. Beaver, S.J.

**1831**   William H. Wall built the first Cuban cigar factory in Key West in 1831, employing 60 workers. His factory opened the doors for a flood of Cuban migrants seeking freedom from Spanish oppression. The population of Key West had now increased to 517. This emigration of Catholic Cubans changed the religious demographics of Key West to the point of compelling the vicariate to recognize their need for a priest.

**1832**   The Territorial Council replaced the town charter of Key West with an incorporated city charter authorizing the election of a mayor, six councilmen, and real estate taxes. In 1834 a private school was established; free public schools were not available until 1870.

**1835**   In September of this year the first recorded hurricane of any intensity struck the island. There were fewer than eight hundred people on the island and most of the damage was to ships in the harbor. During the aftermath of the storm, Key West was basically cut off from the outside world as there was no telegraph and mail service was monthly. Our community was left in the hands of God and to its own resources to recover.

### The Second Seminole War 1835-1842

The Second Seminole War began in 1835 with the refusal of certain tribes under the leadership of a young warrior, Osceola, to be relocated to western reservations (the Trail of Tears). Also known as "The Florida War", it was a conflict from 1835 to 1842 and is referred to as "The Seminole War".

This conflict was the most expensive Indian War fought by the United States and lasted longer than any other war involving the United States from the American Revolution to the Vietnam War.

**1836**     On January 6, 1836 a band of Seminoles attacked a plantation on the New River, in present-day Fort Lauderdale, causing residents of the New River area and of the Biscayne Bay country to flee south to Key West. On July 23 of the same year Seminoles attacked the Cape Florida lighthouse, severely wounding the assistant keeper in charge, killing his assistant, and burning the lighthouse.

**Chief Osceola / Billy Powell**
**(PD-art)**

Approximately two hundred refugees sought refuge in Key West, increasing our population to 600. These attacks put all of the Keys' settlements on high alert since they were so accessible to Indian raids from the Everglades. Even though there had been recent sightings of natives, the settlers of Indian Key, the county seat of newly created Dade County, chose to stay on the island to protect their property. They possessed a small militia with six cannons and were relying on the protection of an established naval base on nearby Tea Table Key.

On the morning of August 7, 1840, a large party of 'Spanish' Indians raided the island: killing, looting, then burning the buildings. Of the approximate fifty people living on the island, forty made their escape; among the dead was Dr. Henry Perrine, a well known physician and director of the Tropical Plant Company of Florida. Ironically, Dr. Perrine had moved there from the mainland with his family for fear of Indian hostilities. His wife and three children were able to make their escape through a trap door in the floor of the house and remain hidden in their turtle crawl while the good doctor disguised the door from above.

Today, an unincorporated community between Homestead and Miami is named after Dr. Perrine, who in 1839 was granted land by the United States Congress for his service as United States Consul in Campeche, Mexico. This grant was given to support his plans to introduce new plants from tropical countries into cultivation in the United States. It is possible that our Key lime evolved from the Mexican lime which Dr. Perrine introduced to South Florida.

**1844**     In 1844, Bishop Portier placed the Parish of St. Augustine and the missions of East Florida (which included Key West) in charge of two French Fathers of Mercy, the Rev. Benedict Madeore and Rev. Edmond Aubril. The Catholic population in Key West was then estimated at perhaps 15 families, numbering not more than 100 from the baptismal, marriage, and funeral registers of that year. Sacramental records of this community only date back to 1842 as earlier records were destroyed by fire.

## Florida the 27th State

**1845**      At the conclusion of the Seminole Indian War, Florida began to grow and it was soon clear that it was time for the territory to become a state. There was much discussion on whether it should be considered one state or two, but congress determined that it should be one. On March 3, 1845, President Tyler officially signed the bill designating Florida as the twenty-seventh state.

Great Seal of Florida
Public Domain

The military importance of Key West was recognized by the government and so the construction of Fort Zachary Taylor began in 1845; the following year the completed work was destroyed by a powerful hurricane.

Flag of 1845
by BJBernreuter

## The Great Havana Hurricane

**1846**      The storm began its approach on Saturday, October 9th of 1846, with light squalls and rain. These increased in intensity throughout the night and by Sunday the 10th, it had developed into a full blown gale with fierce winds and constant rain. On this Sunday the first recorded Mass was being celebrated in Key West by a visiting Havana priest. The Mass took place on the second floor of City Hall, a two story building, at the foot of Duval Street. Erected over the water, the first floor being a fish and meat market, one can imagine the sound of the waves crashing beneath the building, the howling wind, and the dark gloom that must have hovered over the entire island.

This was the eve of the Great Havana Hurricane of 1846, which would strike Key West a devastating blow. There was no government weather service or means of advance warnings. No phones, no telegraphs... no way to know of the devastation that was occurring only ninety miles to the south and heading their way.

When it arrived the following day with winds exceeding 134 miles per hour, the killer storm, a Category Five by today's ranking, destroyed the Sand Key Lighthouse and the Key West Lighthouse, taking the 20 lives of those seeking shelter within them. The death total in Key West was fifty and the storm damage exceeded $200,000 in 1846 dollars with 594 buildings being destroyed or severely damaged. The Settlers' Cemetery on the southwest shore was destroyed and many bodies were washed out to sea with the storm surge.

As of this writing, the U.S. Weather Bureau rates this as the second strongest storm to ever strike our country, the Labor Day Hurricane of 1935 being the strongest.

**1847**     The Settlers' Cemetery was removed from the southern beach area to the center of the island where it remains today.

The continued buildup of federal military installations on the island steadily increased the number of Catholics. By 1847 it was clear that the Catholic residents were in dire need of a church and a priest. Aware of the island's needs, Bishop Portier sent Father James A. Corcoran, a newly ordained Irish priest, to Key West, where he remained for several years.

**1848**     A joint resolution of Congress in 1848, approved by President Polk, recognized claims of the Catholic community of St. Augustine, for church property confiscated by the government at the cession of Florida from Spain. These claims were submitted for arbitration to a prominent Key West attorney, Stephen R. Mallory. Mallory examined documents and interviewed numerous people in Havana and St. Augustine before rendering his decision. His research found that the true owner of the properties in question at the time of cessation was the Spanish Crown, therefore their title had been legally conveyed to the United States Government.

U. S. Military Cantonment.     1. Warehouses and Wharf of F. A. Browne.     3. Warehouses and Wharf of F. C. Greene.     4. Warehouses and Wharf of O. O'Hara.     5. Duval Street.     6. Front Street.     7. Fire Engine Hou
8, Fleeming's Key and Naval Anchorage.     9. Turtle, Crab and Fish Market,     10. Blacksmiths Shop.     11, Tops of Cocoa Nuts North of the Warehouse.

THE BUSINESS PART OF
**KEY-WEST.**
Looking North.     Reduced from a pencil sketch by W. A. Whitehead  Taken from the Cupola of the Warehouse of Messrs. A. C. Tift & Co.,     June 1838.

**Drawing Courtesy of the Library of Congress  (PD art)**

This 1838 map of Key West depicts the waterfront at the end of Duval Street. It shows about a third of the city existing at that time. Wall Street is almost in the center going from the bottom of the picture towards the upper left. The parallel street to the right is Front Street. Duval Street is almost centered horizontally, going from right to left, it is shown in blue. Duval Street is not shown clearly, but is directly in front of the large warehouse in the center of the picture and ends at the water between the small fire house and the two story warehouse on the other side. That is the two story house that may have been the location of City Hall.

# Chapter 4
## The Oldest Parish

**1850**   The Seventh U.S. Census, taken in 1850 showed Key West, clearly the largest city in Florida, with a population of approximately 2,600 residents of which 10% were estimated to be Catholic.

In 1850, under the direction of Pope Pius IX, the state of Florida, east of the Apalachicola River, was transferred from the Diocese of Mobile to the newly formed Diocese of Savannah, Georgia, under Bishop Francis X. Gartland, its first bishop. Shortly thereafter the new bishop's attention was drawn to the growing Catholic community of our island. Responding to this community's request, he sent Father John F. Kirby to Key West from Savannah. That same year, 1851, Father Kirby immediately set about constructing the first Catholic Church in Key West on Duval, between Eaton and Fleming Street.

**1852**   The land had been purchased from Mr. Hiram Bennett for the sum of $266, and the deed was consummated on the 31st of January 1852. This would be the third Catholic Parish erected in all of Florida and the first and foremost in South Florida. The U.S. Census of 1850 lists it as one of only five Catholic Churches in all of Florida. (St. Augustine of course is the oldest parish established in 1565, followed by St. Michael's in Pensacola, established in 1781.)

The first Catholic Church

Amid great ceremony and with solemn decorum, the church was dedicated on the 26th of February, by the Right Rev. Bishop Francis Xavier Gartland. He was assisted by Rev. Edward Quigley of Macon, Ga., and the sermon was preached by the Rev. Jeremiah W. Cummings S.T.D (Doctorate in Sacred Theology), of New York. With the established boundaries of the parish bordered by the Atlantic Ocean on one side and the Gulf of Mexico on the other, the dedicated title of "St. Mary Star of the Sea" was a perfect choice.

This was an exciting event for the whole community, for never before had the island been graced with such an ecclesiastical entourage, as this was the first time a bishop had ever visited the Keys.

In addition to the pageantry of the dedication, the bishop also confirmed two groups of children, the first on February 9th and then another on March 14th.

According to Jefferson Browne, *Key West the Old and the New*, "This church had among its early congregation many black families, some free and some slaves, belonging to Catholic families from St. Augustine. For them was assigned a part of the church separated from the whites." (p.34) The fact that black people were church members was unique to the Catholic parish as most of the other churches on the island maintained a whites' only congregation.

(PD old)
**Bishop Francis X. Gartland**

The Catholic population numbered about 300 and among the early parishioners of St. Mary Star of the Sea, were members of the following families: Alderslade, Baldwin, Bowyer, Clark, Connell, Cook, Fagan, Driscoll, English, Gandolfo, Gannon, Grillon, Gunn, Haley, Logan, Madden, Mallory, Mead, Mulherin, Noonan, Savelli, Wall, and Walton.

That November, Father Kirby was recalled to Savannah and on the 8th of the month, Father Joseph N. Brogard was appointed our resident pastor. Assisting him was Father Edward Quigley, and in 1853, Father J. T. O'Neil arrived. Father Brogard was also given charge of the mission churches in Tampa and in Tallahassee, a feat made possible by the *Gulf Coast Schooner*.

Much of the city's wealth and growth which had depended upon the wrecking industry, was to undergo a formidable change as the government began the construction of a series of reef lighthouses in 1852.

**1853**     Either in 1852 or 1853 a tower with a small bell was erected on the church grounds and persons of all faiths listened regularly for the mellow sound of the Angelus, which was rung three times daily.

In 1853 the first rectory was established on the church grounds. It was housed in a building which had originally served as a slave barracks. This building was owned by Dr. Daniel Whitehurst, a noted physician, who donated it to the church.

**1855**      A true and faithful servant of Christ, Ellen Mallory passed on to her heavenly reward, after many years of devoted service to her church and community. During the mid-fifties an outbreak of yellow fever took its toll on the priests who arrived to continue the work of the parish. As fast as one came, he was stricken and another would come to take his place, only to succumb to the dreadful fever. In 1854 Father Edward Quigley served as pastor, and in 1855 Father Edward Murphy and then Father John Barry served as pastors.

Then in 1856 Father J. F. Kirby returned with Father Clemens C. Prendergast, SPM (Society of Fathers of Mercy) to administer the sacraments.

**1857**      Bishop John Barry of Savannah, visited Key West and administered the sacrament of Confirmation to a small group of children. He was accompanied by Father Prendergast and Father Edmond Aubril, SPM. Bishop Barry appointed Father Aubril to remain as temporary pastor. This same year saw Stephen Mallory elected to the U.S. Senate where he served as Chairman of the Naval Committee.

Pope Pius IX created the Vicariate Apostolic of Florida in January of 1857 and named Augustin Verot the Vicar. As a Vicariate, Florida was separated from the Diocese of Savannah and given a more or less independent character, although it remained a missionary district under the final supervision of the Roman Congregation of the Propagation of Faith.

When named to the Vicariate of Florida, Verot tried to decline the appointment and the episcopacy by citing poor health, age, discomfort in the heart, and the fact that he "always wanted to live and die a Sulpician." However, both his Sulpician superior in France and Archbishop Francis P. Kenrick of Baltimore persuaded him to accept the new responsibility out of obedience. At the age of

St. Mary Star of the Sea collection (PD art)

**Bishop Augustin Verot**

53, he became the first prelate from the American Church to reside in Florida. He arrived on June 1, 1858, at his vicariate headquarters in the former Spanish colonial city of St. Augustine.

When Verot arrived in Florida he found three parishes and seven mission chapels, and only one was in South Florida: Key West's St. Mary Star of the Sea. There were no schools, no convents, and no Catholic social service institutions. He had three priests, two Frenchmen of the Society of Mercy and an Irish diocesan priest. This accounted for the whole Catholic presence in Florida.

**1859**     In 1859 the Parish of St. Mary Star of the Sea, even without a priest, was assigned the new missions of Tortugas Island, Fort Myers, and Tampa. The population of the island at this time was slightly less than 3,000. The Bishop conveyed his inexpressible grief that he was unable to grant a resident pastor to the many places which asked for one with such earnestness, as Key West, Tampa, and Tallahassee.

In 1858-59 Father J.J. Cabanilla, Fr. Marius Cavalieri, and Fr. Felix Ciampi, all belonging to the Society of Jesus (Jesuits), officiated at Key West in the absence of a resident pastor. They were probably only visiting priests or here on a special mission, as Father Ciampi was a renowned preacher in Philadelphia at that time. The Jesuits of Cuba were also invited to attend Key West monthly during the vacancy. The Metropolitan Catholic Almanac of 1859 states that "... a priest here would find a very good support."

### Sisters of the Holy Names First Visit

This was also the year that twelve Sisters of the Holy Names of Jesus and Mary, Archbishop Francis N. Blanchet, and Rev. J.B. Brouillet were bound for the Oregon Territory in a cargo ship, *The Star of the West*. Stormy seas greeted their approach to Key West where Capt. Harrison cast anchor in the harbor and announced a day of respite from the rocking vessel. Heralding their arrival a military salute was fired from the fort in honor of General Winfield Scott, of Mexican War fame, who was on board. They refreshed themselves in Key West and were drawn to a little frame, cross-mounted church where they gave thanks to God for His divine protection.

The Sisters found that the only sources of education on the island were two private schools operated by John Bethel and Miss Euphemia Lightbourne. If parents were unable to afford the tuition their children were deprived of a formal education. They reported back to their Order in Montreal that the people of Key West were uneducated and untamed. This inspired their Superior General, Mother Theresa of Jesus, who was brimming with missionary zeal, to write to Bishop Verot concerning the lack of educational opportunities in this parish under his jurisdiction. This seed dropped by the wayside did eventually bear a blessing and nine years later, Bishop Verot would request that the Sisters open a school in Key West for the education of girls.

The following narrative by one of the Sisters gives us a glimpse into their day on the island and a firsthand description of the interior of our original church. Note that the sister refers to Key West as Thompson's Island, a name given it by Lieutenant Perry back in 1822. The sister writes:

So many natives, dressed in a peculiar garb attracted our attention and we were soon surrounded by a motley crowd who gazed at us with no ordinary curiosity. We directed our steps to church... (which) is built of wood, small but neatly kept. An oil painting of the Blessed Virgin, two smaller pictures and the Stations of the Cross make the interior decorations. There is a small gallery containing an organ of proportionate dimensions which resounding melodies under the touch of Sister Mary Calvary, formed an accompaniment to the voices of the Sisters.

On leaving the Church we found it surrounded by people, many of whom asked to go to confession. Rev. Father granted their request and promised them Mass at 4:00.

The following morning... Devotions being over, a good Spanish woman invited us to supper. We made the round of the island. An old lady, hearing that there were many priests and religious on the island came in all haste towards us and asked us to come and bless her children in her house.

Thompson's Island is one of nature's favored spots; the vegetation is most luxuriant, flowers and fruit growing everywhere. The inhabitants enjoy their island home but they are deprived of the consolations of religion. Visits of the priests are of rare occurrence. Father went to say Mass at the little chapel. The anchor is to be drawn at 5 o'clock a.m. At 3 o'clock we pass Cuba.

On May 14, 1859, Verot sailed for France in order to seek priests for Florida. He succeeded in recruiting seven secular priests, among them was the young Father Sylvanus Joseph Hunincq. Father Hunincq was assigned to Key West in February of 1860. His efforts at administering to the sick and dying, in complete disregard for his own wellbeing, quickly won the love and devotion of not only his parishioners, but the entire island. He often made trips to the Tortugas islands to comfort the soldiers and prisoners and administered the sacraments to the ill at the Key West Marine Hospital.

Father Hunincq is credited with the following inscription that was found inscribed on a plaque beneath a painted likeness of Our Lady Star of the Sea:

**"Since it first shed its light in Key West,**
**it has like a star of the sea to the wandering mariner,**
**been a star of hope and comfort in times of despair and sorrow,**
**and a star of joy to those who have lived in its teachings."**

Father Hunincq died that summer of yellow fever after having ministered to so many during the epidemic of that year and was buried in the Catholic Cemetery. A marble slab was inserted into the wall of the church to commemorate his life and services as he was loved by people of all denominations for the great catholicity of his charity.

**1860**     Mainly due to the wrecking industry, Key West was now the largest, wealthiest city in Florida and the richest city per capita in the United States. In 1860 the population of Key West stood at 2,900 while Fort Dallas (Miami) was just eighty-three. Ft. Dallas was a post where missionaries could visit with the Seminole Indians and Bishop Verot, concerned about their spiritual welfare, promised an effort would be made to visit them from Key West. For years to come, Key West would be Miami's lifeline to the world, as the rest of South Florida would remain an untamed wilderness.

## The War Between the States

**1861**     By February 1861 (before Lincoln took office as president) seven southern states passed secession ordinances and were followed shortly afterwards by four more. The Civil War began April 12, 1861, when Fort Sumter in Charleston, South Carolina was attacked and captured by the Confederate Army. President Lincoln immediately federalized 75,000 militiamen. In July, the Union Army under Gen. Irvin McDowell suffered another defeat at the First Bull Run, 25 miles southwest of Washington. The Confederate General Thomas J. Jackson earned the nickname "Stonewall" as his troops turned back the Union Army.

**1862**    On January 31, 1862 President Lincoln issued General War Order No. 1 authorizing the Union Army to begin hostilities against this Confederacy.

During this conflict a new ironclad navy, driven by steam power, blockaded the non-industrial south in an effort to put a strangle hold on its replenishment of arms and much needed supplies. The efforts of the war strengthened and unified the industrial North while wreaking havoc and disruption throughout the South. Although Florida was one of the original seven states to withdraw from the Union, Key West, like other major Florida ports, was held by the Union Navy throughout the war.

Key West, considered the most strategic Union port within the southern states, was a determining factor in the outcome of the war as it held more naval vessels than any other U.S. port. The Eastern Gulf Blockading Squadron stationed here was responsible for capturing 299 blockade runners, impeding the flow of arms to the southern states through the Gulf of Mexico.

In August 1862, the Rev. F. Ciampi, S.J. returned to Key West and with Fr. Joseph M. Eneiro (Encisio?), S.J., served until December, when Father James Hassan arrived as rector. He was succeeded in 1864 by Father Joseph O'Hara, who left shortly before June of 1866, when Rev. Henry P. Clavreul, Florida's grand old missionary, visited the island. He was succeeded by Father A. O'Mailley, who served from 1865-1866. Whereas most citizens were strong Confederate sympathizers, many families were torn when husbands and sons went off to war on opposing sides. How difficult it must have been for the priests here administering to such a divided community.

**(PD old)**

**Rev. Henry P. Clavreul**

Fort Zachary Taylor 1884
Map courtesy of the Library of Congress. (PD old)

# Chapter 5
## Catholic Reconstruction

**1865**      The Civil War brought disaster to the South in the forms of poverty, dislocation, and the disruption of any semblance of government to its people. Even though he supported the Confederate cause, Bishop Verot maintained a vision for Florida Catholicism. In 1866 he suggested the creation of the Diocese of St. Augustine for the whole State of Florida, including the territory west of the Apalachicola River which belonged to the Diocese of Mobile. This division was not to come to pass for another five years.

Reconstruction was a time of fundamental social, economic, and political change. Besides the cost of material rebuilding, the spiritual impoverishment caused by war, defeat, and financial destitution, also required a moral regeneration. But funding for revitalizing the church was not readily available and Verot had to beg for financial assistance from the northern bishops as well as the Society for the Propagation of the Faith in Lyons, France.

Verot planned a spiritual reconstruction by two means: the establishment of private Catholic schools for blacks, and the introduction of parish missions. In 1866 Florida law allowed for the education of black people but it was never enforced. In addition, before 1869, all education in Florida was through private schools. Education, especially for black children, was a priority to Bishop Verot. In 1867, at his urging, the St. Joseph Sisters of Le Puy (his home town) came to St. Augustine to establish a school for the black children. Key West was very much a part of his program and he would soon be requesting help in setting up schools on our island for both white and black children.

"The second component of Bishop Verot's spiritual reconstruction was the introduction of parish missions (a popular revival of Catholicism done at the local parish by a priest from outside the parish and usually lasting a week)." (McNally, 1982, p. 10) He invited the Redemptorists to Florida, to conduct missions in the parishes, including St. Mary Star of the Sea in 1869 and 1870.

Bishop Verot visited Key West on many different occasions and during his first visit to the island, just after Christmas of 1865, Bishop Verot sailed to Fort Jefferson on Dry Tortugas and said Mass for the prisoners. Following the Civil War the fort had been used as a federal penitentiary and one of the inmates who made his confession to the Bishop was none other than Dr. Samuel A. Mudd. Dr. Mudd had been imprisoned for complicity in the assassination of Abraham Lincoln. He was convicted for setting the broken leg of the assassin, John Wilkes Booth during his escape attempt.

While in Key West, the good bishop visited the tomb of the much loved and missed Fr. Sylvanus Hunincq, stating that something would be done to honor his memory. He left for Tallahassee on Jan. 2, 1866 encountering a severe storm on his passage but arriving safely none the less at St. Marks on the Epiphany of Our Lord, Jan. 6th.

**1866**   Towards the end of May, Bishop Verot again visited Key West, following a begging tour through Rhode Island, Connecticut and Montreal. Arriving on the steamer ship *Liberty*, he spent ten days on the island and confirmed a number of children. He also purchased a small house and lot at the rear of the church from a Mr. William Whitehurst for $700.

Rev. JP. Allard

St. Mary Star of the Sea Collection

From 1866-75, Rev. Jean-Baptiste Allard, OMI (Oblates of Mary Immaculate) a French-Canadian missionary, was assigned as pastor to Key West. Fr. Allard was a good friend of the Sisters of the Holy Names and would be influential in their coming to Key West.

During his tenure, the International Ocean Telegraph Company laid the cable connecting Key West to Cuba and also the mainland of Florida. Can you imagine… sending a note to the bishop and (possibly) getting a response that same day?

**1868**   Cuba's struggle for freedom from Spain was ignited by Carlos Manuel de Cespedes, a distinguished lawyer and wealthy Cuban planter who gave the cry, "Cuba Libre" from his estate, La Demajagua, near Manzanilla. Regarded as the first Cuban patriot to raise the cry for freedom, his followers subdued the Spanish garrison at Bayamo, exposing the inadequacies of Spain's military to oppose the brewing revolution. In retaliation, Spain recruited the lowest of society as volunteer militia. They were given free rein to put down the revolution by any means possible. Thus began the Ten Years War (1868-1878). The atrocities committed against the populace forced more Cubans to emigrate, for both political and economic reasons, and settle in Key West.

**C. M. de Cespedes**
(PD art)

The United States maintained neutrality during this unsettled period, but this did not prevent the local Cubans from converting their hard earned wages into guns and supplies for the rebellion. These were transported on fast, American owned, private vessels known as "filibusters".

The year 1868 was also a landmark year for the church in South Florida, when Bishop Verot sent the following letter to His Grace Ignace Bourget, Bishop of Montreal:

Your Grace,

A letter from Father Allard coming from Key West informs me that your Grace is now in a position to send a small group of Sisters of Jesus and Mary to Key West to aid the missionaries in their work of regenerating the religious and moral life of the island. I cannot tell you how much pleasure the news gave me, and I hasten to express my gratitude to your Grace. The work of the priest cannot be completed without the cooperation of these good religious, who are destined to give good mothers of families to the nation.

We willingly accept all the conditions laid down by your grace. Regarding the item that specifies that the house and grounds shall be the property of the sisters, we will endeavor to give satisfaction. A large house and lot have been purchased. Father Allard has not told me in whose name the titles are to be held, but there will be no difficulty.

Father Allard tells me that the school year is now quite advanced; - a fact that causes me concern - however, it is true that if the sisters came now they would find themselves soon in the extreme heat of summer - which, without preparation, might have bad results. It would be better, then, to wait until next October. Before that time I hope to have the opportunity of making a little visit to Canada.

Permit me to thank you once again for your kindness, to recommend myself to your prayers, and to offer you my respectful homage.

Augustin Verot, Bishop

The good Bishop also sent a letter to the Mother House in Montreal requesting their Order to open a school for girls in Key West. This next excerpt is from that letter conveying the hoped for results of such a school.

*Believing with the illustrious Bishop Spalding that members of the Catholic sisterhood, with their spirit of self-sacrifice, their courage, their eagerness to follow in the way of pedagogical progress, were best fitted to cultivate in the hearts of Key West's young women the virtues which are a woman's chief glory, and lacking with no degree of mental culture can make her beneficent and delightful. That is the Sister's chief aim to inculcate, pure mindedness, modesty, patience, piety, reverence, gentleness, amiability and helpfulness is conceded by friend and foe, for on such a foundation must we build if we would raise woman's mind to the ethereal height of intellectual trust, without risking the loss of her heart, of goodness, and of love.*

I wish that I could detail every letter and word exchanged between the Mother House, Fr. Allard, and Bishop Verot. That becomes a book in itself. However I have chosen certain entries that summarize and show the willingness, cooperation, and spirituality of all involved. The following is an excerpt from a note from Fr. Allard to the Sister's Community dated September, 21, 1868, *"Our Lord will be, Himself, the host of the first pioneers and will transform their exile into a Fatherland."*

The Sisters respond, *"In such wise does He present the healing balm of His sweetness even before He makes his own taste the bitter chalice of sacrifice."*

### Sisters of the Holy Names of Jesus and Mary

The following five Sisters of the Holy Names of Jesus and Mary were then chosen ending a great anxiety amongst all the sisters: Sister M. Euphrasie was named Superior and accepted her burden with courage; selected to accompany her were Sister M. Octavie, Sister M. Angelique, Sister M. Pierre, and Sister M. Monique. Sister M. Euphrasie, experienced in leadership, with good business acumen, and dependable in a crisis, was well chosen to lead this group to an island on the very edge of the frontier of Catholicism. Being transferred to Key West was considered an exile of sorts, entailing a difficult journey with little promise of creature comforts or timely communication with the mainland.

This small community of sisters, with Rev. H. Landry assigned as Assistant Pastor, travelled via railway from Montreal to New York on October 15, 1898. The next day they boarded the steamboat *Sedwidge*, the only freighter leaving New York en route to Texas, with a stopover at Key West. The captain of the vessel, Mr. Cuildergale, was a non-Catholic, at first he remained distant towards the sisters, but his demeanor improved and eventually he became their friend.

They set sail on the 18th and within a few days were in the grasp of a raging storm. On October 22nd the captain reported that all masts were carried away by wind and sea and so declared the ship abandoned to the will of the waves. The Sisters prayed to Mary, under her title **"the Star of the Sea"** for safe conduct. Their heartfelt prayer was answered as the storm slowly subsided. They were now very anxious to arrive in Key West.

How often we are battered by the storms of life, especially as we embark on new endeavors to serve Our Lord and God. Is it Satan challenging our courage, trying to put us off our mission; or does it come from God to test our resolve and strengthen us for the battles ahead? Maybe it is a little of each.

The Sisters' entourage arrived in Key West on October 24th, thankful to have survived the storm. Upon disembarking, the Sisters were heartily welcomed by all the residents as education for their children was of paramount importance. They were greeted by Fr. Allard and brought to the church where they opened their hearts in the presence of their Dear Lord. There they offered themselves to Him, to work for His Glory on this isolated island.

[**Author's Note:** The ill-fated *Sedwidge* encountered another storm in the Gulf of Mexico a few days after departing Key West and was lost with its entire passengers, crew, and cargo. The captain and his first mate alone escaped and lived to tell the Sisters of the misadventure at a later date. Captain Cuildergale, though he was a Protestant, saw the finger of God in these events and gave the Sisters the title of "Protecting Angels" during the storm. He was certain that had the Sisters remained aboard the ship, it would not have perished.]

Upon leaving the church the Sisters were separated into two groups. Three of the Sisters would reside with the family of Dr. Whitehurst, whose house stood next to the Catholic Church, on the corner of Eaton and Duval.

Sister M. Pierre

St. Mary Star of the Sea collection (PD old)

Sister M. Octavie

Sister M. Angelique

(Where the old McCrory's Five & Dime used to be located). The other two were guests in the family home of Capt. George Alderslade. His home was located on the other side of the church (where the La Concha Hotel stands today).

The city at that time was primarily located between Southard and Front Streets, with most of the buildings already occupied. Whitehead Street, which was the only path passable from one end of the island to the other, had been cut by sailors from the US Sloop *Concord* in 1846.

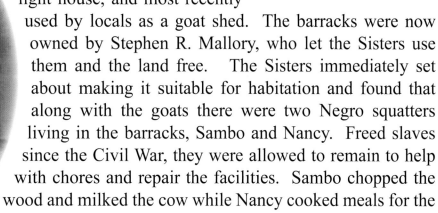

St. Mary Star of the Sea collection (PD old)

Sister M. Euphrasie

The only building available for their use was the abandoned Civil War Union Barracks, opposite the light house, and most recently used by locals as a goat shed. The barracks were now owned by Stephen R. Mallory, who let the Sisters use them and the land free. The Sisters immediately set about making it suitable for habitation and found that along with the goats there were two Negro squatters living in the barracks, Sambo and Nancy. Freed slaves since the Civil War, they were allowed to remain to help with chores and repair the facilities. Sambo chopped the wood and milked the cow while Nancy cooked meals for the Sisters.

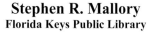

**Stephen R. Mallory**
**Florida Keys Public Library**

A detached building, two stories high, the barracks contained nine rooms. On the ground floor they placed a chapel, a parlor, a music room, a refectory, and a drawing room. Upstairs was divided into classrooms, a community room, and a dormitory for the children. Porches surrounded the house on all sides. Portions of it were boarded up to create rooms for a choir, a sacristy, a kitchen, and cells for the Sisters. Their bed consisted of an iron bedstead with a simple mattress made of moss. They reportedly slept well enough after a hard day of work.

On the 29th of October, a picture of St. Rose of Lima (patron saint of Mother Marie Rose Durocher the founder of their order) mysteriously appeared on the wall of the new community room. One of the Sisters noted that, "One should not question how Our Lord intervenes in our lives, just acknowledge that He does."

Civil War Union Barracks
Monroe County Public Library (PD old)

With volunteer help and financial assistance from the community, the barracks were ready for the first students within a month. Not wasting any time, they opened the school for white girls on November 7th, with twenty-six young women enrolled. Thus the first Convent of Mary Immaculate, the oldest educational institution in South Florida, had its humble beginnings in a framed government building.

Mallory subsequently deeded the property to Bishop Verot on December 8th for the sum of $200; fifty dollars less than he paid for it in 1847. Verot then conveyed it to Rev. Mother Marie-Stanislas, Superior General at the Mother House in Montreal. According to their agreement, it was given to the sisters with the understanding that if they ever abandoned the convent established there that the property would revert to the Diocese.

### The First Vatican Council 1868

The First Vatican Council was convoked by Pope Pius IX on 29 June 1868, and our good Bishop Verot was called to Rome to participate. He was a very active participant in the council proceedings and was described by one historian as the "enfant terrible" of the council for his frequent and lengthy speeches. One of the more significant doctrines produced by the council was its definition of Papal infallibility, but it was also marked by a debate on the rights of Negroes. Bishop Verot insisted that the church take a strong stand for racial justice. He wished the council to condemn the theory that Negroes did not have souls and proposed a canon forbidding the assertion that Negroes were not of the human family.

In late November of 1868 Bishop Verot again visited our island bringing with him Fr. Sartorio. Bishop Verot was the guest of Father Allard and Father Landry, who had accompanied the Sisters of the Holy Names. He spent more than a month here, there being no boat available to sail home. While here, the good bishop purchased a plot of land, 300 by 300 feet, for the sum of $1 from the city. Bordered by Francis and Angela Streets in the city cemetery, it was to be used exclusively as a Catholic burial ground.

**1869**    In the summer of 1869, Father J. E. MacDonald, stood in for Father Allard who left on a mission to Canada. Only hours after Fr. Allard departed, Fr. MacDonald was struck down by yellow fever while officiating at the second Mass and had to be helped from the altar. He died a short time afterwards. Only twenty-six years old and well loved by the whole community, Fr. MacDonald had become afflicted while serving the spiritual needs of the yellow fever patients. It was his ministry to be at the side of the sick and dying, offering the consolations of our faith and preparing them for the great change awaiting them in their new life. It was lamented that many a sailor and many a soldier would feel that the hospitals had lost a zealous priest and they, a good and kind friend.

He was buried in the Key West cemetery. It was expected that Father Encisco, SJ, would arrive from Havana in time to perform the last services but his steamer arrived too late. So at the insistence of the locals the services were held by a layman and the good Sisters of the convent.

Father Landry had been sent to Tampa, so Fr. MacDonald was replaced by Father Encisco when he finally arrived from Havana, Cuba, but six days later, he also died of yellow fever. Yellow fever soon spread across the island and forced the closing of the school. Two more Jesuit Fathers came over from Havana, Father Avignon and Father Nubiala. On August 16, 1869, Father Avignon also fell ill and died of yellow fever, then Fr. Nubiala returned to Cuba leaving Key West with no priest. A priest was finally sent from the Savannah Diocese to assist until Fr. Allard returned from Canada.

To honor the memory of these missionary priests in Havana, Cubans set aside a beautiful burial plot in Colon Cemetery and erected an exquisitely sculptured monument to them. The name of one of the principal streets in Havana was also changed to Padre Varela, to honor one of the priests who died in St. Augustine, Florida. An early advocate of self-rule for Spanish Colonies, he was condemned to death by King Ferdinand VII in 1823 and immigrated to the United States.

[**Author's Note:** Father Felix Varela was decreed "Venerable" by our Holy Father Pope Benedict XVI, on Easter Sunday, April 8, 2012.]

Remember, all this occurred during the first outbreak of hostilities in Cuba. Certainly, with such a healthy mix of Spanish and Cuban immigrants living in Key West tensions were high. Eighteen years earlier, May of 1850, violence had erupted on our island as some of the 'unruly' Cuban liberators, under Narciso Lopez, looted stores belonging to Spanish families.

In Cuba, those suspected of sympathizing with the "liberators" were threatened with arrest and kept under watch. Even though he was a Spaniard, Señor Vicente Martinez Ybor supported the Cuban cause and was accused of providing funds to Cuban rebels. Fearing for his business, Ybor decided to move his entire cigar manufacturing business from Havana to Key West. This brought whole families, mostly Catholic, from Cuba to live and work here. Other leading Cuban cigar factory owners quickly followed his lead. Soon Key West became the largest Clear-Havana handmade cigar center in the U.S.

That year Sister M. Angelique also succumbed to tuberculosis, probably worsened by yellow fever, and was the first of many sisters to die here due to climate and tropical disease. She was buried next to Fr. MacDonald in the city cemetery. The school later reopened with its second enrollment of 134 students, 16 of them boarders. During the time of the school's closing, the Sisters depended on the charity of the community, both Catholic and Protestant, who never failed in their support when the Convent needed help.

Father Allard returned in October with four more Sisters of the Holy Names and a new assistant, Fr. Paul LaRocque. Father Allard established a parochial tuition-free school for white boys, to be supervised by the Fathers and taught by the Sisters. Sister Mary Theophile and Sister John of the Cross, who had recently arrived, taught there from 1870 to 1872, when Mr. W. J. Chappick would assume that responsibility.

**St. Mary Star of the Sea Catholic Church on Duval Street.** St. Mary Star of the Sea collection

# Chapter 6
## A New Diocese

**1870**      Following up on Bishop Verot's suggestion five years earlier, Pope Pius IX established the Diocese of St. Augustine on March 11, 1870, with the French Bishop (Verot) its first Ordinary (an ecclesiastical term used to denote a local residential Bishop who has canonical jurisdiction over persons and things of a diocese). Technically, Florida was no longer an ecclesiastical frontier on the "Rim of Christendom". However, the challenge for Catholics in South Florida changed very little. How was the parish to cope with the lack of funding and shortage of clergy, while at the same time expected to provide basic Catholic services, such as schools, to ensure the survival of a small and fragile flock?

Key West at this time had a population of 5,657 and with the cigar industry, sponging, wrecking, and fishing, it was considered a bustling metropolis compared to other Florida cities.

As predicted, the good Sisters' presence here was producing immediate rewards for the Kingdom. Reverend Gross, a Redemptorist, gave a mission in February which was attended by Dr. Whitehurst, who had hosted the sisters on their arrival to Key West. After the mission, on February 15th, the doctor was baptized by Fr. Gross, fulfilling a promise made to Sr. Angelique as he attended her in death the previous year. Impressed by her faith and goodness, he had promised to convert to Catholicism which had been his deceased wife's religion.

The Army Major General F. W. Sherman, a relative of the more famous General W. T. Sherman of Civil War fame, was stationed here with his wife and small son. The family also received baptism in the Convent Chapel and in March of 1870 he and his wife received their First Holy Communion. He was a devoted friend of the Sisters and upon his departure in 1871, he presented them with his carriage and a span of handsome horses. His only request was that his long cherished horses would always have a groom and a driver who would appreciate them and treat them kindly.

Mother Marie-Stanislas, Superior General of the Sisters of the Holy Names, purchased a lot fronting Duval Street, from the estate of William H. Wall, for the sum of $200, extending their grounds from Whitehead along Rocky Road (which was locally called Military Road, then officially named Division Street by the turn of the century, and now known as Truman Avenue) all the way to Duval. (This is the location of Appel's) This gave the Sisters ownership of one half of the block bounded by Truman, Whitehead, Olivia, and Duval.

Although the black people of the South had been freed of the yoke of slavery, they were unable to advance much beyond their former economic level due to the lack of an education. This did not deter our great Bishop Verot, the Sisters of St. Joseph, or even the Sisters at St. Mary Star of the Sea. Therefore, at the request of Bishop Verot and with the support of Fr. Allard, the Sisters opened a tuition-free diocesan school for the black children. In return for their services, the pastor supplied a much needed resident chaplain for the students and the Sisters at the Convent school.

Thanks to the local chapter of Masons who donated the Odd Fellows Hall, five children registered on the first day. This gesture of concern from the Masons for the education of the blacks seems to be unique to Key West, as reputedly, this organization was anti-Catholic and anti-immigrant. Regardless, it was generously given and graciously accepted by these Catholic Sisters from French-speaking Canada.

Sr. Augustin was the first teacher at this school. She was joined the next year by Sister Damien. Unfortunately the school had to close temporarily due to a lack of enrollment and a lack of funds.

This year the first school bazaar was held and raised $815 for the church renovations.

**1871**     St. Mary Star of the Sea Church was repaired, enlarged, and a large pipe organ was installed. The parish was then honored as the first stop on Bishop Verot's whirlwind tour of the diocese that he began just after Easter in 1871. He proceeded to Tortugas and then on to Havana, where his journal shows that he found the "old records of St. Augustine documenting three hundred years."

The fruits of the Sisters' works are again demonstrated with the departure of Miss Mary Kelly to Canada as the first religious vocation to come out of Key West. Upon taking her vows she took the name of Sister Angelica of Mary.

The first graduation exercise for the Convent of Mary Immaculate was held that year. Miss Annie Alderslade, later to become Mrs. C.B. Sweeting, was the only graduate. This was not unusual during this era for any city or school much less one so small and recently established. In fact the first graduate from the public school of Key West occurred 37 years later, in 1908, and J.L. Lester was the only graduate in that class.

The Cuban Club Ateneo, now in its second year, re-organized under a new name, "The San Carlos Club", named after Cuba's Seminario San Carlos, a renowned educational institute of higher learning in Cuba. Its purpose was to raise support in Key West for the revolution now brewing in Cuba.

**1872**   Since it was the only Catholic Church in South Florida, St. Mary Star of the Sea maintained the records of the baptisms and marriages conducted by Father DuFau, who was sent from Bishop Verot to minister to several Catholics in March of 1872 "in a place generally known as Miami". Priests from this parish also acted as chaplains for Army and Navy personnel stationed at Key West, as well as for the crews of naval vessels that docked at the port. In later years, the Navy would provide their own chaplains to handle this responsibility.

A smallpox epidemic occurred in Key West in 1872, forcing the schools to close from January 16 to March 4th. The disease was so rampant that marines were stationed outside of quarantined homes. Four of the good sisters offered their assistance to the city council. Sister Mary Monique and Sister Mary Octavia were the first to accept the ministry to act as nurses and as they neared exhaustion, Dr. Whitehurst insisted they take a rest. Sister Mary Maurice and Sister Mary Germaine then took up the charge and followed them into quarantine, moving into the ten square foot shanty built for them by the city on the beach. This had been designated as the "Pest House" and was near the hospital. Other Sisters in turn nursed the sick, most of whom were the black families. In early March the epidemic ended and the nuns returned to the convent and reopened the school. In a show of appreciation for the Sisters' efforts during the epidemic, Mr. Blake's band serenaded the Sisters at the Convent.

**1873**   Bishop Verot visited Key West and confirmed about 70 persons on the first stop of his diocese tour in April of 1873. In July of that year Sr. Theophile was struck by lightning but was protected by the Blessed Virgin and was unharmed.

Sister Theresa of Jesus arrived in August as the new Superior of the convent. Sr. Theresa of Jesus was one of the five original nuns of this order founded by Blessed Mother Marie Rose (Eulalie Duroucher) in 1844. In 1857, Sr. Theresa became the third Superior General of the Mother House and served in that office until October of 1867. She was then elected to Assistant General.

In response to the steady increase of the Cuban population Mother Theresa quickly opened Our Lady of Mercy School for Cuban girls. The school was dedicated to St. Theresa with Sr. Irene and Sr. Theophile, both fluent in Spanish, serving as their first teachers.

**1874**   Father Allard died in 1874 and was buried in the city cemetery, so in the absence of Father LaRocque, who had left to finish his studies, Father A. F. Bernier, his assistant, was left in charge. Sister Theresa chose Fr. Bernier to replace Fr. Allard as Chaplain to the Convent which apparently caused some hard feelings with Fr. LaRocque who wished to retain that ministry.

Trouble with Spain continued to fester as it was openly known that the rebels were being supported by American and local Cuban interests. The Spanish capture of the filibustering vessel *Virginius,* and the subsequent execution of 53 of her crew and passengers, many who were Americans including the Captain, brought the tensions to a boiling point and the U.S. prepared for war. Combinations of U.S. fleets from around the nation were assembled in Key West, totaling 26 ships. Forty thousand troops were said to have landed on South Beach for drills in preparation for a Cuban invasion. Having some 10,000 residents at that time, this would have been quite a cultural and logistic shock to the island city. Spain agreed to pay $80,000 to the families of those killed to avoid the conflict, but ill will between the two countries intensified.

**Fr. A. F. Bernier**
Patrick S. Scott collection

When the school reopened it continued to increase in enrollment until it became obvious that a larger facility was needed. The tenacious Mother Teresa of Jesus was not one to sit around and wait for someone to do something, so she sold the convent school and both lots to the Leland Hotel Company for $5,000 with the understanding that it could continue functioning as a school until the new convent was built.

She then purchased eight and a half acres from the John P. Baldwin estate taking ownership in her own name. The property was outside the city limits at that time and fronted on Rocky Road (Truman Ave.) bordered in the rear by Virginia Street, and taking most of the two blocks between Simonton Street and Windsor Lane.

The actual sale was concocted by Amelia P. Baldwin, the widow and administrator of the estate, who petitioned the Court to provide a commissioner to sell the land at public auction. Attorney George G. Watson conducted the proceedings at what amounted to a private auction for the agreed upon sum of $1,000. There were no competing bids against the Sister's offer as generally everyone knew of the arrangement between the Sisters and the Baldwin family.

The money was to cover attorney fees, probate, and other title obligations. In gratitude to the Baldwin family, there was supposedly an unwritten agreement that no descendant of that family would ever pay tuition at the school.

This land was totally unimproved and filled with trees and underbrush which needed to be removed. Because she wanted a beautiful convent, Mother Teresa, along with two auxiliary Sisters and a few workmen began to clear the land by hand. However, the workmen balked, as they were convinced the property was

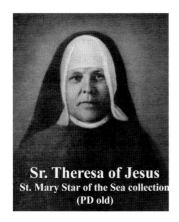

infested with venomous snakes. Mother Theresa, making the Sign of the Cross, took up her sickle and proceeded to clear the brush. Her courage inspired the workers to do the same. She dug up rocks, removed useless shrubs, and pruned the fruit trees. She saved any plant that would embellish the approach to the convent. The other Sisters would help during after-school hours and on the weekends.

One cannot appreciate the efforts of these nuns without observing them in their full length wool habits, shawls, layers of undergarments, and their headdresses, visors, and veils. With only their face and hands uncovered, they would toil alongside any worker. Unlike you and me, they only had two sets of clothing, so washing of garments was a nightly chore after each day's work. And they did not have washing machines or dryers. They worked for room and board (provided by their own labor). Through their work and devotion they earned the respect and love of the community.

**1875**    On January 14, 1875 the foundation of the new Convent of Mary Immaculate was laid and construction commenced. The architect for the convent was an Irishman by the name of William Kerr, who relocated to Key West in 1872. He would later design and build the Monroe County Courthouse and City Hall in 1890, and then Federal Customs House in 1891.

Resembling a building Kerr had known in France, the convent walls were constructed of native stone quarried from government property on the island. The stone was obtained free of charge through the efforts of George (Claude) Babcock Sr., an Army Engineer, who arranged for the Sisters to receive the stones, excavated for construction of Army installations, without any cost other than the labor of those who did the work for the quarry.

In February, Mother Marie-Stanislas, the Superior General, visited the community. After touring the grounds and recently laid foundation of the new convent she reported back to the Mother House:

*"The new building, plans of which bear the stamp of Mother Theresa's genius, will not be habitable before one year. The site chosen, some 800 acres in extent, on which coconut palms and other trees are planted, is one of the most beautiful in the city."*

The Rev. Joseph L. Hugon was sent here by Bishop Verot in 1875, as acting pastor and remained until 1877, when Father Paul LaRocque returned. Father Bernier continued as his assistant until tensions between him and Fr. LaRocque caused him to be reassigned the following year to a post in Tampa.

Bishop Verot's last visit to our island occurred the Easter of 1875. He gave a retreat and confirmed 71 parishioners. Verot also gave the habit and renewed the profession of some of the Sisters of the Holy Names. He then went to Miami to visit the Indians and a new chapel which had been built for them there.

Another yellow fever epidemic broke out on July 22, 1875 and forced the good Sisters to move into the uncompleted convent building. Two days later the first Mass was held in it. The experience moved one Sister to write:

*"The building is octagonal in shape forty by forty feet with wings fifty feet hung on either side. According to the plan the octagon part of the building will be three storied in height and wings two stories by the dormers. At the moment, as we take possession, the outside walls are only two storied high and only one wing is roofed. The openings have neither doors or windows but are closed only with rough wood. When completed the building will be magnificent. The proportions are a grandiose scale..."*

In September when only thirty-six children arrived for school Mother Theresa purchased a horse and wagon to pick up the children at their homes.

Construction of the Convent restarted when the yellow fever left, but was halted again on November 15, 1875 due to the lack of funds. The completed construction cost of the first building was $35,000, so two sisters were sent on a begging tour to New Orleans and Jacksonville to raise money. They often endured humiliating rebuffs and returned with only $250.

Monroe County Public Library (PD old)

Bishop Verot visited the Wagner homestead in Miami in 1875, holding services in their home. He administered the sacrament of Confirmation to members of their family. The Catholic congregation of Miami consisted of four members of the Wagner family and a nearby settler, Mr. John Adams. The good bishop promised William Wagner that if he were to build a church a priest would be sent annually to conduct services. William accepted and built a fine chapel next to his home, measuring twenty by forty feet.

This was the first house of worship in Miami and one year later Fr. Hugon travelled from Key West to dedicate the chapel. Fr. Hugon stayed with the Wagners for more than three weeks. And so it went every year as reported in the Diary of George Parsons in Miami who wrote: *"Arrived from Key West, a boat with a load of bananas and a Jesuit. The priest set off walking to Wagner's house."* This was a four mile walk up river. A week later Parsons' diary noted the priest's return.

**1876**      The St. Francis Xavier School for black children reopened six years after the first school had faltered. Set on firmer footing it would serve the black community for 86 years. Sister Augustin was once again put in charge and assisted by a lay teacher.

In January, Mother Theresa of Jesus and Sister Irene went to Havana to beg from the families of their Cuban students. She returned to her Mother House in Hochelaga and found herself embroiled in a brouhaha with the diocesan authorities. Bishop Verot had sent a letter of complaint concerning her to the Mother General Sr. Stanislas; the "Congregation's Ecclesiastical Superiors" had decided not to let her return to Key West. It turns out that Fr. LaRocque had sent a terrible report concerning her leadership abilities to both the Mother House and to the bishop. She was devastated and soon surmised that it concerned her role as the Sisters' Superior in Key West and Fr. LaRocque's interference with their autonomy. Following the example of Blessed Sr. Marie Rose, the foundress of her society, Sr. Theresa had more than once put herself on the line to correct excessive demands made by certain priests. Now she would suffer the consequences. The Convent was finally completed in 1876 and enrolled 300 students.

The Chronicles of the SNJM of January 16, 1875 totally contradict Father LaRocque's accusations and state:

**"Our devoted Mother Theresa, let it be said to her praise, did not hesitate to use axe and rake, herself, as she labored to speed up the construction of the convent. She drew up the plans herself. We can certainly say that she was the soul of this difficult enterprise".**

The Chronicles of June 13, 1876 add the following praise of Sr. Theresa:

**"...who devoted several years to this mission. The new building, which she planned and had constructed, will always be a monument to her courage and her tireless zeal. The Sisters who saw her clear the land with her own hands could speak eloquently and truly of her spirit of sacrifice and her devotedness..."**

These eyewitness reports show an entirely different lady than the one described in LaRocque's letters, however he was pleased with the results and expressed his satisfaction for the change in administration in Key West.

The beloved Bishop Verot died on June 10, 1876, leaving a legacy of a true shepherd. He had led his flock through a very difficult era of loss and regrowth. The whole state grieved at his passing. His successor was an Irishman, Bishop John Moore.

On October 19th, a weak hurricane crossed the island with little damage. The significance of this storm was the local ability to predict its arrival because of the works of Rev. Benito Vines, a Jesuit priest and director of the meteorological observatory of the Royal College of Belen, in Havana, Cuba. His studies of cloud movement and falling barometric pressures had shown that one could predict the course and intensity of approaching storms. Known as "Father Hurricane" his forecast techniques became known as the "laws" of Father Vines and they laid the foundation for our present hurricane warning system. Father Vines published his work, *Ajpuntes Relativos a los Huracanes de las Antilles,* the following year. It was reprinted in English by the U.S. Army Signal Corps' national weather service. The U.S. Weather Bureau was not yet established.

State Archives of Florida
floridamemory.com/ show/142807 (PD old)

The Sisters' chapel which occupied the entire 2nd floor of the convent's eastern wing.

This map from 1884 will show you the landscape of the period. You can easily make out the new convent #1. In the upper right #2 is the Union Army Barracks that housed the Sister's first school. #3 lower left corner is the first Catholic Church on Duval St. You should be able to identify other landmarks such as Hemingway's House (built in 1851 by Isa Tift), the Light house, AME Church, etc.

Map courtesy of the Library of Congress. (PD old)

53

**1877**    Father LaRocque returned to Key West and had as his assistant, Father J. M. Fourcard, who died of yellow fever the following year and was also buried in Key West.

**1878**    Our Lady of Mercy School for Cuban Girls, opened in 1873, was closed because of low enrollment and the financial burden of the convent construction. The building was sold for $400. Enrollment in all three schools had declined so much that the Cuban girls were combined with the American girls at the Convent of Mary Immaculate.

**1879**    Sisters Theophile and Augustin return from a successful begging tour in Havana. They managed to acquire $3,110 for their efforts.

By 1879 there were so many Cubans in Key West seeking freedom from Spanish rule, that Father LaRocque erected a Cuban chapel, Nuestra Senora de la Caridad del Cobre, (Our Lady of Charity del Cobre), for them on Duval Street, between Division Street (Truman Avenue) and Virginia Street. The chapel was popular as long as there were priests available to staff it, but by 1898 it was closed. It was moved later to its present position on Windsor Lane.

Two Jesuits, Father Avenione and Father Encinosa, came to Key West from Havana to assist the priest, and they also died of yellow fever. At this time Father Spandenari became the new assistant to Father LaRocque.

St. Mary Star of the Sea collection

**Fr. Paul LaRocque**

The following letter is a rare glimpse into the past, documenting current conditions at the time of Father LaRocque's tenure as pastor. The letter was sent to Bishop John Moore, who sought to organize the administration of the diocesan parishes by requiring an annual report (notitiae) from every pastor beginning in 1878. This letter was in response to an inquiry concerning the first such report from St. Mary Star of the Sea. LaRocque does not reveal the questions, but lists the question's number in the left hand column and proceeds to answer it. However, one can easily ascertain the questions considering his responses. He does make reference to having spoken to the bishop and appending informative notes to the Notitiae. The transcription of his letter has kept true to the spelling and punctuations of the original and is in a font very similar to his handwritten Victorian style.

Question 1°	The Church of St. Mary Star of the Sea in Key West was dedicated in February 1852, and Rev Joseph N. Brogard appointed its 1st Pastor, Nov 8th 1852 by Right Rev. F.X. Gaitland Bishop of Savannah. I do not know of any Parish documents on record showing the condition of the Mission at that time, number of Catholics?? An idea of its progress may be formed from the following statistics. There were registered in

| 1852 | 43 | baptisms |
| 1853 | 10 | " |
| 1854 | 14 | " |
| 1860 | 23 | " |
| 1870 | 100 | " |
| 1878 | 126 | " |

The progress of the Mission may also be seen in the establishment in 1868 of a school for white girls, one for white boys in 1870 and one for colored girls in 1874 _ There were over one hundred heretics converted to the Catholic Faith from 1870 to 1879.

The war of secession, the impossibility of keeping a Priest continually residing here from 1852 to 1869, and finally the death of four Priests by yellow fever May be mentioned as the principal vicissitudes through which the Mission had to pass

Question 8°	Key West with a population of about 14,000 inhabitants, Chocolaski population about 30 Miami or Fort Dallas Key Largo Dry Tortugas or Fort Jefferson vacated at present, and hundreds of other places called Keys most of which are, to this day, uninhabited.

The population of Key West as to its origin is divided into three principal elements: British, Spanish and American_

Question 9°	All are supposed to be civilized. Quite a number of

converts have already been made as above stated, from the ranks of english speaking Protestants,_ A great many, especially among the young girls who have attended our convent school, would soon become Catholics if not prevented by the strong, blind opposition of their parents_ I consider that there is hardly any hopes of more conversions being made among the present generation that is those already settled in active life and the old ones gradually dying out _ The future progress of Catholicity here among dissenters, must be limited almost exclusively to the rising generation. As to the Spanish speaking population of this Mission, I have already acquainted you by word of mouth and by notes appended to the Notitiae, with their religious condition _ Anything more I might say, would not substantially add to the value of the information now in your possession.

Quest. 11°      About 9000 nearly all heretics plus 4000 Cubans who, though baptized Catholics, never practiced the Catholic faith.

Quest. 12°      About 600 that is the proportion of 1 to 21 to the non Catholics.

Quest. 13°      Strong inducements continually held out to Catholic men and women to join secret societies, which, they are told, will secure them work situations & I have counted 37 names of English speaking Catholics belonging to secret societies_ Heretical books and immoral news papers of every description, circulated through the efforts of Protestant propagandism ┐

Quest. 14°      8 protestant meeting houses _3 public free schools and perhaps half a dozen private schools. I am not aware that there is any particular effort made in those schools to pervert Catholic children_ There has been a good deal of that devilish work carried on in The past I am told, when there was no residing Priest here _ But now the devil has some kind of

fear of <u>holy water</u>

Quest. 15°    Most of the Catholics under my charge are located in Key West_ Those of Chocolaski are grouped together on the small island of that name, 60 miles north north east of Key West_ At Miami, about 120 miles north east of Key West, and Fort Meyers about 150 miles north of KW. the few Catholic families are scattered in every direction with an intervening distance of some times ten and fifteen miles which had to be traversed in buggy (?") or saddle.  Visits to those differents parts from Key West, must necessarily be irregular and attended with quite an amount of tediousness and fatigue, as none but sail vessels (some very small hardly offering any shelter against a scorching sun) can be depended on

Quest. 17°    Five: Key West, Fort Jefferson whenever U.S. troops garrisoned there Chocolaski, Miami and Fort Meyers

Quest. 19°    Two: one in Key West, the others at Miami, on the right bank of the Miami river, about one mile from its mouth.

Quest. 20°    The Blessed Sacrament is kept in the Chapel at Key West, and in the room used as a Chapel at the Convent, with all the exterior respect and decency possible under the circumstances of poverty we live in.

Quest. 21°    Two Priests, both foreigners (you might put me down as a Turk)

Quest. 31°    Regular meetings of societies of men and women at which the Priest has the opportunity of expounding and inculcating the principals of the Christian doctrine
A Benevolent Society of Ladies who hunt up the poor in their sickness and whilst assisting them in their bodily wants, try also to prepare the way for the Priest to the bed side of the dying sinners.
Dogmatic instructions given every Sunday in the evening

for the special benefit of Protestants and ignorant lukewarm Catholics.

Also Catechistical instructions for children every Sunday afternoon in Church_

Quest. 32?      Trinkets might do for Italians and Cubans, but I think they would be a failure among Americans.

Quest. 33?      Besides what I mentioned under question 13?     I would add that another great obstacle to the progress of Catholicity is to be found in mixed marriages especially if it is the mother that happens to be Protestant. Few mixed marriages have been performed since there is a Priest residing here_ But I find there has been quite a number of them previous to 1870 and in almost every instance where the mother is not Catholic the children are brought up Protestants or bad ignorant Catholics.

An other obstacle to the progress of Catholicity is to be found in the necessary and continual contact of Catholics with and their dependence for a livelihood on Protestants who form a very great majority of the population. We naturally feel inclined to think, speak and act like those whom we associate with_ The French proverb says very truthfully: "dis-moi qui tu hantes et je te dirai qui tu es." Wince I look upon it as an almost hopeless task to succeed in inculcating Catholic principles and enforcing Catholic practices among Catholics so disadvantageously associated.

Finally I would mention as an other great obstacle to the progress of our holy Faith the impossibility of supplying those whose minds are poisoned by bad reading, with the proper antidote found in good books offered (at least the use of them) gratis _ I say gratis, for there is such a fearful indifference to good, solid Catholic reading that I believe

that where one hundred young folks would willingly pay a dime for a dime novel, ten would hardly be found willing to pay a red cent for a good moral pamphlet.

I do not see the use of entering here into any particulars as to how such obstacles could be removed, in as much as the main power by which the proper remedies to those crying evils might be procured, money, fails entirely here in the poor missions of this land of flowers.

Catholic free schools are not possible if we judge by accomplished facts, even in thoroughly Catholic places, much less are they possible among a class of Catholics so deficient in Catholic spirit and material resources_ Flourishing Catholic Societies, for the keeping of Catholics together and the spread of Catholic principles, are very fine things to talk about. But have to maintain them, if established, where a few dozens of members at most can be relied upon, and where new members could scarcely be induced to join even if offered a premium for doing so?

I would say let the Prop. Of the Faith Bureau increase tenfold the allocations usually made to such poor Bishops as is the Bp. Of St. Augustine, and then with the hearty cooperation of his Priests I feel certain that nothing will remain untried that might be accomplished for the preservation and growth of the Catholic Faith in this portion of the Lord's Vineyard, once purpled with the blood of martyrs.

P. LaRocque

Key West Fla
July 25th 1879

In this letter, LaRocque mentions a place he calls Chocolaski over by Fort Myers. This small island is correctly spelled Chokoloskee, and was settled by a few Italian families, hence the reference to using trinkets to entice the Italians and Cubans, but not the Americans.

Also of peculiar note is the population he states for Key West, of 14,000, which is fairly close to the present day population of the island. It will surprise many to learn that his numbers are correct. Key West at this time was one of the largest cities in Florida if not the largest. By the turn of the century it was also the richest city per capita in the United States. Fr. LaRocque lived in a very industrious, busy, and metropolitan environment here. The cigar industry was flourishing as was the wrecking industry. Miami, also known as Fort Dallas, was nothing more than a defunct fort left over from the Indian Wars, a relatively small fishing village.

The French quote, LaRocque uses in his treatise, **"dis-moi qui tu hantes et je te dirai qui tu es."** is a popular French saying which translates as: *"Tell me who you associate with and I will tell you who you are."* Or as Americans would say, *"You are known by the company you keep."* Father LaRocque would eventually become Bishop of Sherbrooke, Canada.

**1880**     Sister Angelique's remains were removed from the city cemetery and reburied in the new cemetery for the nuns on the Convent grounds. From 1880 to 1886, Father Felice K. Ghione, an Italian priest, had charge of the church without any assistant until Father Ronald B. MacDonald, SJ, arrived in 1887.

The heirs of Simonton gifted a tract of land commencing at the intersection of Simonton and Virginia, to Bishop Moore, in April of 1880. (It is now occupied by the Duval Square businesses.) The next year, 1881, St. Joseph's College for white boys was established on this property by the Sisters of the Holy Names of Jesus and Mary to replace the boys' school which the priests had started back in 1869. Classes were held in a small house on the property.

**Fr. Felice K. Ghione**
St. Mary Star of the Sea col.

**1884**     A gas plant was constructed in back of Emma Street, which extracted a poor quality gas from coal, which was then delivered through underground iron pipes to homes and businesses to fuel gas lamps. This was a very inferior product which produced little light and a lot of smoke.

**1885**    The first streetcar franchise was granted and began operation with a mule team pulling the cars along rails on the main thoroughfares of Key West. By the turn of the century this would be converted to electric trolleys. Key West was a very up and coming city with all the modern conveyances.

State Archives of Florida, Florida Memory, http://floridamemory.com/items/show/5050

**1886**    The worst fire in the history of the island struck March 30, 1886. Suspiciously it began at the San Carlos Institute which housed the Cuban School and Cuban Consulate's Office. Founded in 1871 and known as "Casa Cuba", it had become the local symbol of the Cuban revolution. It was never proven that the fire had been purposely set to weaken the resolve and finances of the local Cuban sympathizers, but rumor was that Havana newspapers had reported Key West on fire three days before it happened.

Monroe County Public Library    (PD old)

The fire raced through town destroying nine cigar factories, the tobacco warehouse, and the cigar box factory. Churches, homes, six wharves, and five brick warehouses were destroyed.

Because wood was the primary building material on the island, such that even the roofs were of wooden shingles, and because the buildings were placed so close together, the fire spread quickly from rooftop to rooftop, until over one third of the city was in flames. Unfortunately, at this same time the only fire engine the city owned, a horse drawn steam engine, was in New York undergoing repairs.

Our church was located in the heart of the fire district, only one block from its origin. Miraculously, St. Mary Star of the Sea was spared and can be seen in the upper left corner of the photo. Ever conscious of the needs of the community, the children of families who were stricken by the fire were allowed to continue in Catholic schools without tuition.

March 1, 1886, a new building was constructed as a school for black children, boys and girls, on the lot facing Virginia, between Simonton and Duval. It was dedicated by the pastor, Rev. Paul LaRocque and placed under the patronage of St. Francis Xavier.

Later that month the Sisters boarded the battleships anchored in the harbor to beg for alms. Ferried from ship to ship, they received $281 from the sailors. These men were not making much money in 1886, only $20 - $30 a month, so this was probably a good amount for their efforts.

St. Francis Xavier School
Monroe County Public Library (PD old)

**1887**   In October an eight foot tall metal statue of the Blessed Virgin Mary arrived and was placed in the 4th floor façade of the Convent. It was a gift from the workmen who built the school. Each Saturday every man would make a contribution from his weekly wages for the purchase of the statue. I am sure that working alongside the Sisters earned them more in blessings than just their take-home pay, and this gift was a token of their esteem for the piety and humble service the nuns were providing this community.

**1888**   In 1888, the new St. Joseph's School for young boys was erected on the corner of Virginia and Simonton, next to the existing St. Francis Xavier School of which it was similar in design and construction. Separated by a small fence, the children of different races played next to each other.

Monroe County Public Library (PD old)

**1889**   Suffering the loss of many of his diocesan priests to the scourge of yellow fever and cholera, and faced with a shortage of local vocations, Bishop John Moore was desperate to find priests. He looked to his native Ireland, seeking to recruit young seminarians, but there were not enough. The populations of Tampa and Key West were expanding due to the immigration from Cuba and in dire need of spiritual guidance. With nowhere else to find help, the Bishop turned to the Jesuits of New Orleans and offered them the missions of South Florida.

Thus on July 31, 1889, after an absence in Florida of 146 years, Bishop Moore and Rev. James O'Shanahan, the New Orleans Provincial of the Jesuits, signed an extraordinary document which gave the Jesuits "exclusive and perpetual rights" to the missionary territory.

The agreement was so unusual and unfavorable to the diocese that at first the Vatican authorities were reluctant to approve it. The only place not offered to the Jesuits was Key West, where the Italian Diocesan Pastor, Father Felice Ghione, was canonically irremovable until he wished to leave.

This agreement, made with good intentions, was unworkable from the start. Thirty years later Bishop Michael J. Curley would rectify the agreement.

**1890**    The 1890 census showed Key West as the largest city in Florida with a population now at 18,080 citizens. Mr. John J. Philbrick acquired the controlling interest in the coal plant and established an electric lighting plant which would eventually end the production of gas. There was an old saying in Key West that we were the second city to have electric service and the last to have indoor plumbing.

Father D. Bottolaccio, a French priest, arrived that year to assist Fr. Ghione. Fr. Bottolaccio was just returning from visiting his home country and then Rome, where he had received an audience with Pope Leo XIII when he was assigned to Key West. He is credited with forming a chapel, Our Lady of the Nativity, and small school for Cubans in 1892. His familiarity with the Spanish language enabled him to bring back many Cuban adults to the church. During the cigar workers strikes of 1894, he extended aid and spiritual comfort to those in need.

The San Carlos Institute was rebuilt on a spacious lot, at its present location, fronting Duval Street in the heart of Key West in 1890. This was a two story wooden structure.

**1897**    Sister Louis Gabriel arrived in Key West having just pronounced her vows. She would teach regular classes at the school as well as music and art. This began her 51 year tenure in Key West where she remained until her death in 1948.

The Sisters' journal reported that during this year every sister contracted yellow fever, yet none perished. The Blessed Mother and her Son watched over these good women with protection and grace. A nun's life at the convent revolved around the students, service to the community, and devotions. How did they do it and still find time to feed and clothe themselves? Well, they raised chickens for eggs and meat. They had cows to milk and a garden where vegetables and fruit were grown. They had a community dining hall where they would gather to eat the meals prepared by the nuns who were not certified for teaching. They relied on cisterns and wells for water. Bath water had to be carried up to the fourth floor of the convent. They had a laundry room on the grounds which is now serving as the meeting hall for the Knights of Columbus. It resides next to the Sacred Heart Hall. All washing was done by hand and hung out to dry on a clothes line. Their appearance was impeccable, hoods and collars starched, habits pressed and spotless, shoes always sporting a shine. Their personal effects were few, as they had taken vows of poverty.

Of course they could not attend to those personal needs until the classrooms had been swept clean, the yards attended to, and the school's hundreds of doors and windows secured. Do not forget their daily devotions and prayers. Each night allowed a short time for community and writing to their families. So now you know how they survived: through tenacity, love, and faith in God's providence. Convent records indicate that there were 609 students registered that year.

Father Ghione returned to Italy in 1897, on account of ill health, and advised Bishop Moore that he would not return to Key West. Because there were not enough diocesan priests to serve the 10,000 Cubans in Key West and Tampa, a second contract had been signed by Bishop Moore and Rev. O'Shanahan, the Jesuit Provincial, in 1891 and mentioned the handing over of Key West "In Perpetuum" to the Jesuits. With Fr. Ghione's departure, Fr. Bottolaccio was recalled to St. Augustine and St. Mary Star of the Sea entered a new era.

**Convent Entrance**
**State Archives of Florida**
floridamemory.com/show/67374 (PD old)

# Chapter 7
## The Jesuit Era

**1898**    The first Jesuit pastor, Rev. Anthony B. Friend, SJ, arrived in Key West February 15, 1898. A native of Switzerland, he had served as a missionary in Alabama and Georgia for 15 years and most recently served as Pastor of St. Louis Church in Tampa. His assistants here were Father L. Schuler, SJ, and Father P. Faget, SJ.

Father Friend, SJ
St. Mary Star of the Sea
collection

He would have been exhausted from his journey down the coast and eager to unpack and settle into his new home, but that was not to be, for this was graduation night for the class of 1898 of the Convent of Mary Immaculate. Graduation ceremonies were being held in the restored San Carlos Opera House and the new pastor's presence was required.

The Valedictorian, Miss Sybil Curry stated as part of her address, ***"...what if life have dark days? One sunlight is ever learning, the light of religion to which, like guide, instruct and console, but above all she must endure..."*** How prophetic her words would soon become; in a very short time the dark days would descend upon them and the Sisters' endurance tested beyond their imagining.

During the ceremony a loud explosive noise was reportedly heard and witnesses claimed that the building literally shook. They heard shouting on the streets, "Maine blown up; Maine blown up!" The town was in an uproar up and down Duval Street. Sister Louis Gabriel noticed how upset the audience was and called Key West's only policeman, who was standing outside the door, to come in and calm the crowd down. He was able to reassure everyone that all was safe and the disaster was an accident in Havana, 90 miles to the south. The graduation then continued in spite of the near riot occurring outside.

Having come from Tampa, Father Friend would have been well informed of the mounting Cuban skirmishes occurring across the Straits of Florida, but probably not prepared for the interruption of this night's festivity when word was received of the sinking of the Battleship *Maine* in Havana Harbor.

This event ignited the Spanish American War, which would last less than four months and bring an end to the Spanish rule in Cuba, but leave a permanent mark on the citizens and institutions of this community. Many Cuban crusaders had visited Key West to raise funds and support for their cause, among them were General Melchoir Aguerra, Maximo Gomez, and lately

José Martí, considered the "George Washington" of Cuba. Inspired by Martí, this island had become inflamed with a passion for a free Cuba and by all accounts everyone knew it was just a matter of time before someone or something would spark the revolution. For many in Key West the sinking was personally tragic as the U.S.S. *Maine* had been in and out of our harbor for more than a year with the officers and crew taking an active part in our island's social life. There were many friendships formed and everyone anxiously awaited news of who had survived.

**José Julián Martí Pérez**
courtesy of John M. Kennedy T.
(PD old)

The Lighthouse Tender *Mangrove,* under command of Captain P. L. Cosgrove, was the first U.S. vessel to arrive on the scene in Cuba. He would later turn over the *Maine's* flag, its commission pennant, and many other articles rescued from the battleship to the Sisters in the convent. These would later be displayed in the convent museum.

For the next two weeks many of the *Maine's* victims, injured and dead, were being returned to Key West. They filled the antiquated Navy Marine Hospital and the Barracks Hospital at the Army Post. Then the "reconcentrados" began to arrive. These poor victims of the Spanish oppression managed to make it across the straits starving and in rags.

Realizing that there would not be adequate hospital facilities on the island once war broke out, Mother Mary Florentine, the Superior of the Convent, called together the Sisters and presented a plan to them. She proposed to close all the schools and turn the buildings over to the government and volunteer themselves to nurse the sick and wounded. Despite their lack of medical training, it was unanimously agreed upon, but they would need the approval of the Mother House in Canada. Mother Mary Stanislaus, Superior General of SNJM, gave approval under these conditions:

First: There was to be no remuneration from the United States government for use of the buildings or for the services of the Sisters.

Second: The buildings must be returned after hostilities ceased in as good a condition as when they were turned over to the government.

Two days before the formal declaration of war, Mother Mary Florentine approached Commander James M. Forsyth, of the Key West Naval Station, and placed the Convent of Mary Immaculate, St. Joseph's, and St. Francis Xavier Schools, plus the Sisters' personal services as nurses, at the disposition of the naval authorities.

This offer was relayed to Captain W. T. Sampson, U.S.N. ; he replied:

**"U. S. FLAGSHIP NEW YORK, OFF KEY WEST, FLA.,"**
April 7, 1898.

SIR-
"I. Acknowledging your letter of the 5th instant, stating that the Lady Superior in charge of the schools of the 'Sisters of the Holy Names, Convent of Mary Immaculate,' at Key West, has called on you, and offered, in case of war, to place the convent and two school buildings of the order at the disposition of the naval authorities for hospital purposes, and that the Sisters tender their personal services as nurses.
"2. I cordially agree with your opinion expressed, that this is a most generous and patriotic tender, and beg that you will make known to the Lady Superior, and to the Sisters, my appreciation of their offer, and acceptance in case it becomes necessary.
"Very respectfully,

(Signed) "W. T. SAMPSON,
"Captain U. S. N., Commander-in-Chief U. S. Naval Forces.
North Atlantic Station."

Realizing that the Army Barracks hospital and the Marine Hospital would never suffice once war broke out, the Surgeon General of the U.S. Army accepted the Sisters' offer and on April 20, 1898, the convent, two school buildings, and the grounds of the Sisters of Mary Immaculate, were turned over to the Medical Department of the Army for use as a hospital. The military would refer to it as the 'Army General Hospital', but locally it was known as the 'Key West Convent Hospital'.

Major W. R. Hall and Major S.T. Armstrong, of the Army arrived the next day on the flagship *New York* to convert the convent into a hospital. Sr. Gabriel recalls how they threw up their hands upon seeing all the desks, chairs and other school furniture that had to be cleared out. Mother Mary Florentine stated that all she needed to know was what they wanted done. And they told her how every room needed to be cleared out. Two by two the Sisters went out searching for warehouses and empty buildings and by nightfall they had found enough. The next day with mules and carts they emptied the convent and scrubbed it clean.

When the doctors came back they were amazed at what had been done in two days. The elegant parlor became a drug store; the spacious classrooms of the first floor were converted into wards for the wounded. The second floor was established as operating rooms. Frame buildings were erected on the convent grounds for use as isolation wards, earth closets, etc. and a pesthouse for the

treatment of yellow fever and smallpox cases was established in connection with the general hospital.

Including the two schools, the first floor of the Convent, and 100 emergency tents, they achieved a 500 bed capacity. The Sisters kept only the smallest possible quarters for their own use. In awe of how much the Sisters had accomplished in such a short time Maj. Hall remarked, *"Mother Florentine, in this convent you may be called Mother Superior, but you are really a General of the Army."*

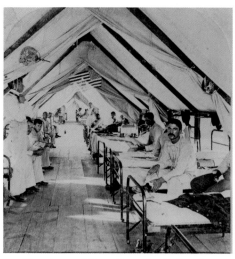

**Courtesy of Joan Langly Collection**

**U.S. Army hospital corpsmen**
**State Archives of Florida, Florida Memory,**
**http://floridamemory.com/show/8674 (PD old)**

Major Hall brought in a staff of nine doctors to man this newly formed hospital: Doctors B. E. Baker, H. P. Jackson, E. G. Ferguson, A. E. DeLipsey, F. M. E. Usher, H. Mann, R. C. Eve, T. A. Clayton, and R. G. Plummer. Major W. C. Borden, Major S. T. Armstrong, and Captain H. A. Shaw were Army medical officers assigned to this facility. Army Nurses assigned here were: Margaret Shaffer, Alice Lyons, Agnes Lease, Jennie Sheerrin, Anna Fox, and Johnetta Sanger. Also included in the staff were 34 members of the Hospital Corps, 9 contract nurses, and 29 employees, cooks, laborers, teamsters, etc. Of course we cannot forget the Sisters of the convent: Sister Superior Mary Florentine, Sr. Mary Theophile, Sr. Simon, Sr. Mary Visitation, Sr. Damien, Sr. John L'Evangelista, Sr. Thomas of Jesus, Sr. Hormisdas, Sr. Laurentius, Sr. Marguerite de Cortona, Sr. Mary Egidius, Sr. Mary Berenice, Sr. Ambroise de Sienna, Sr. Antoine de Jesus, Sr. Dolores, Sr. Catherine de Palanza, Sr. Louis Gabriel, Sr. Anthony, Sr. Maurice, Sr. Domitille, Sr. Gaspard, Sr. Ulderic, Sr. Tharslie, and Sr. Silvestre.

Major W. C. Borden was in charge of setting up the static machine used for the production of Roentgen radiation for fluoroscopic examinations. This would be the first use of X-rays by the U.S. Military for aiding in the removal

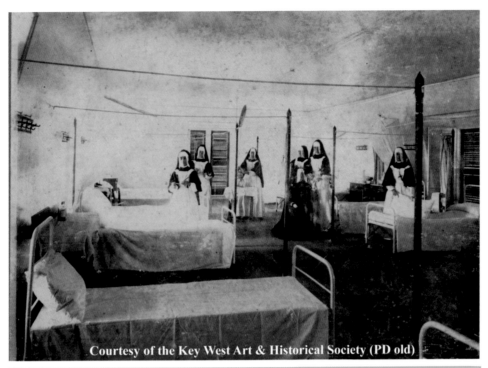

This picture shows a ward of the Convent hospital. The hospital beds and sisters as nurses can be seen. The sisters are Florentine, Simon, Ambrose of Sienna, Anthony, Damien, Palanza, and Hormisdas.

of bullets and shrapnel from wounded soldiers. This technique enabled the surgeons to locate the foreign matter without blindly probing the wounds with steel instruments. Later Major Borden would author *Use of the Roentgen Ray by the Medical Department of the United States in the War with Spain* and many monographs on medical, surgical and military subjects.

During the course of the war, more than 500 wounded were treated at the Convent Hospital. Lt. J.B. Bernodou, commander of the torpedo boat *Winslow*, was the first of the wounded sailors to be treated. He arrived May 12th, the day after the battle in Cardenas Harbor where he was wounded in the left thigh. On July 3rd the decisive Naval Battle of Santiago was fought and for the next two days twenty officers and 306 wounded men were brought to the hospital.

Rev. Chadwick, the chaplain of the battleship *Maine* when she sunk, was also among the first patients in the Key West Convent Hospital. He was suffering from erysipelas when admitted. On recovery he celebrated Mass in the hospital chapel, using the chalice given to him by the crew of the *Maine,* which had just been recovered and returned to him.

Among the non-combatants treated at the hospital was George C. Musgrave, a British correspondent, wounded by shrapnel during the battle of Santiago. Upon his discharge he returned to England where he was knighted by the king.

Clara Barton, founder of the American Red Cross, arrived in Key West from Tampa on April 29th with a group of doctors, nurses, and supplies, all bound for Cuba. Their ship *The State of Texas* was delayed for weeks awaiting clearance to cross the straits.

The Spanish-American War lasted only a few months and was officially over when Spain signed a peace treaty giving the United States control of Cuba, Puerto Rico, the Philippine Islands, and Guam. Cuba, however, became an independent country rather than a U.S. territory.

This is how the Sisters so eloquently described the closing of the Convent Hospital:

*Last Wednesday (August 17), all the sick sailors bade us a last good-by. The "Lancaster" took them on board to bring them to New York. This morning it is the turn of the soldiers and the hospital personnel. Nurses, doctors, as well as the sick, all seemed loathe to leave our hospital, of which, they say, they will always have the fondest memories. The sailors, in good sea language, said it was the best ship they ever were on. The soldiers claimed that no camp compared to it. These testimonies of gratitude chosen out of thousands prove to us once again that the flower of gratitude grows in all climates and in all locations when hearts are generous and noble.*

*At about nine o'clock the wards of the sick were deserted, the last ambulance left our door; and from the hall where we had so often welcomed the sick, we now bade good-by to our dear patients.*

*Since the twenty-second of April when Major R. W. Hall took possession of our Convent in the name of the government to transform it into a hospital, until today, we can but felicitate ourselves on our relations with the thirteen physicians who made up the medical corps; they always treated us with the greatest politeness, and sincerely appreciated our least services. A most cordial understanding existed between us and the fifty-eight secular nurses of both sexes who shared with us the work of caring for the sick. It would take volumes to record all the spontaneous tributes of gratitude received from the five hundred fifty-one soldiers and sailors who came under our care either at the Convent or in the schools. Let it suffice to quote one poor sailor who returned to the practice of religion after many years of negligence. "My stay at the Convent has been my salvation." Several of his companions could have said the same. "How many mothers will bless you for all the good you have done for us!"*

(Langley, 1998, p. 58)

**From Left to Right: Sr. Mary Bernice, Sr. Louis Gabriel, Sister Mary Egidius,**
**Sr. Superior Mary Florentine, Sister John L'Evangelista, Sr. Mary Visitation, and Sr. Thomas of Jesus.**
Courtesy of the Monroe County Public Library (PD old)

After the military pulled out many of the Sisters collapsed from malaria. Their immune systems were most likely weakened from exhaustion. As agreed, there would be no payment from the government for the use of the buildings or the Sisters' services. However the two new buildings erected by the government to provide more space were left on the school grounds. They remained there for two years following the closing of the hospital without any legal or permanent disposition being made by the government. Throughout this time, Mr. M.I. Ludington, Quartermaster-General U.S.A. would petition Elihu Root, the Secretary of War, to take up and resolve this matter. It came down to this: the convent property upon which the buildings were constructed and where the Army mules were kept had been the Sisters' cow pasture. Sr. Florentine, the Mother Superior, was asking that either the buildings be removed and the pasture restored or she would have to charge rent for the continued storage of the buildings on their property. Major Hall endorsed their request to the Secretary of War on Sept. 12, 1898 with these words:

*"Further, I will add but for the great kindness and generosity of this Order it would have been impossible to have established a proper hospital at Key West. The entire amount of this claim, together with the money spent for buildings and alteration, was a small sum compared to the good accomplished by a general hospital at Key West, Fla., where men from both the Army and Navy were sent."*

St. Mary Star of the Sea collection

It would take a special Act of Congress to finally bestow the buildings to the nuns. One building was later used as the Music Hall and the other became the Kindergarten.

When the schools reopened at the end of the war the enrollment was so great that it was evident that additional facilities would have to be provided if the demand was to be met.

An excerpt from a letter written this same year, by Fr. Faget, gives us a glimpse into the daunting challenges the Jesuits were facing in this young parish.

*"The practice of religion among the Cuban population, at least the men, is not encouraging, but the women, as a rule, are better disposed. Our only hope of improving their religious state lies in the efforts made by the zealous Sisters of the Holy Names, seconded by our own, to impart to the children a good Catholic education. Even the American portion of the parish is largely made up of lukewarm Catholics. A great deal of hard work lies before us."*

Sometime in 1899 Father Anthony Taillant and Brother Caspar Heinrich came to Key West to assist Father Friend. Shortly after their arrival there was another outbreak of yellow fever. Father Friend, Father Taillant, and Brother Caspar Heinrich were all struck down. Father Friend recovered and promptly resumed service to those in need. Father Taillant and Brother Heinrich did not recover and died in Key West.

**1900**    With a gift of $700 from the community of Key West, the Sisters established what was to become a very famous museum on the island. It was located on the ground floor, in the rotunda of the Convent. Many relics of the battleship *Maine* and Spanish American War artifacts

The flag and pennant of the battleship *Maine* are displayed.
Photo by Griswold      BJBernreuter collection (PD old)

were displayed along with a plethora of animal mounts and formaldehyde bottled oddities. Old coins, stamps, and other historic collectibles were properly cared for and exhibited. Sr. Egidius was its first curator and was responsible for setting it up. She also taught at St. Francis Xavier for 18 years.

Father T. S. Bamber arrived to serve as Father Friend's assistant in 1900, followed by Father A. J. Brewer in 1901 and Father H. A. Devine and Father M. J. Tiernan in 1902. Utilizing the former Cuban Chapel, the Jesuits opened the Jesuit College, for the higher education of young men, from 1900 through 1916. Later it was discontinued for lack of sufficient patronage.

**1901**     On the 20th of September, 1901, the church that was erected in 1852 by Father Kirby, on the lot on the southwest side of Duval Street, between Eaton and Fleming Streets, was destroyed by fire. As reported in <u>The Florida Times-Union</u> the Haskins family, who were at dinner next door, were the first to sound the alarm. Hearing the noise and seeing smoke, they called in the alarm and shouted "Fire". Father Friend was the first to answer the alarm and rushed inside were he noticed the organ in full blaze. Then a large crowd quickly gathered and many valuables were able to be rescued before the fire forced the men out.

The fire department responded quickly, but the city's standpipe was empty as the water tanks were under repair. They had to remove their steam engines to draw water from the cistern of the Old Stone Church and also the city's cistern. The Navy responded, but their hoses could not reach from the engines to the Church. Sparks were flying everywhere in the stiff breeze and men were obliged to lift buckets to the rooftops of surrounding buildings, some over a block away, to quench the flames and prevent another massive city wide fire.

Every trace of arson was present, as the heart of the fire was in the very center of the organ. There were rumors in later years that the Klan was involved, but the Klan was not re-established until 1915 and there was no active KKK chapter in the keys until 1921, so not much credence is given to this theory today. However, it was noted that a mentally or emotionally disabled man, who habitually hung around the church, was reportedly seen entering and leaving just before the fire broke out.

Although many valuables were rescued from the church much was lost. The Stations of the Cross were salvaged from the debris, but badly burned. One exception was a painted plaque depicting the Virgin Mary as Star of the Sea with the following inscription:

> **"Since it first shed its light in Key West,**
> **it has like a star of the sea to the wandering mariner,**
> **been a star of hope and comfort in times of despair and sorrow,**
> **and a star of joy to those who have lived in its teachings."**
> **Father Hunincq**

Temporary church used after the fire.                    St. Mary Star of the Sea collection

This could well have been the same picture of Our Lady Star of the Sea that the nuns had seen on their first visit to the island. Immediately after the fire, Father Friend started a fund drive to build a new church.

With the church gone, the spiritual focus of the Catholic community centered on the Convent property. The Music Room, one of the two hospital buildings put up by the Government during the war, became a chapel for the celebration of Mass. It was able to hold up to 100 worshipers at each Sunday service.

Father Friend, suspecting that the city would continue to expand towards the east, expressed interest in rebuilding the church in a new location. He was met with resistance from many of the congregation. Some were opposed to the increased expense that would be incurred for purchasing another lot, while others wished to rebuild it on Duval Street for sentimental reasons. After some forceful discussions, Father Friend was able to persuade the congregation to accept the wisdom of moving the church.

Records on file at the Monroe County Court House show that on October 25th, 1901, Father Friend purchased from Tropical Building and Investment Company, a parcel of land fronting 114 feet on Division Street (Truman Avenue) and running along Windsor Lane 488 feet. This was immediately adjacent to

the convent and its school. The sale price was $8,000 at eight percent interest with the agreement that the full amount would be paid off in two years. When the land debt was paid off, Father Friend turned to the task of raising funds for the construction of the St. Mary Star of the Sea Church that stands today. From October 1901, to July of 1905, the whole parish, priests, sisters, and lay people, including some Protestants, supported a drive for a new church. Everyone, both black and white, banded together to raise money. They accomplished this by giving church suppers and holding raffles.

**1903**    Records indicate that in 1903 there were two other pastors who served in Key West, Rev. Wagner, SJ, and then Rev. Tiernan, SJ, along with Father A. Latiolais, who served as assistant. Then, in 1904, Rev. A. Snebelen, SJ, served as a pastor and in 1905 his assistant was Father A.C. McLaughlin and followed in 1906 by Father P.I. Marnane and Father Ina O'Shanahan.

Records are not clear on why other pastors were assigned to Key West during the tenure of Fr. Friend; however it is known that his health was failing during these years and the stress of running the parish may have proved too much.

A boys' high school was opened by the Jesuits in one of the church buildings on Windsor Lane where they continued to educate the young men until 1916 when the sisters were asked to add the high school classes to the elementary school on Simonton Street.

In August of 1903, construction began on the new annex to the Convent of Mary Immaculate.

**1904**    Headline news spreads across the nation that Henry Flagler will extend the Florida East Coast Railway all the way to Key West. There were many skeptics, and always the questions of why and how, which are summed up in this prophetic folk song of the era quoted from Pat Parks' *The Railroad That Died At Sea.*

**Old Solomon Pinder of Knock-Em-Down Key**
    **Puffed on his corn cob and looked out to sea.**
**Word had just reached him of Flagler's great plan**
    **To build to Key West, the ocean to span.**
**'A railroad on land, that's proper,' said he,**
    **'But shiver my timbers! A railroad to sea!**
**If the story be true, sir, mark my words here:**
    **'Twill be a man-killer; the cost will be dear:**
**And many a Conch man will go to his rest,**
    **E'er the first engine whistle is heard in Key West!**

(Parks,1986, p.1)

75

Key West was once again in the national spotlight. Everywhere Flagler brought his railroad prosperity followed. He blazed through Florida building grand hotels along the East Coast for the northern tourist to visit: the Ponce de Leon Hotel in St. Augustine, The Royal Poinciana Hotel and later The Breakers Hotel in Palm Beach, and the Royal Palm Hotel in Miami. He was considered the Father of Miami; when incorporated in 1896 the citizenry wished to name the city "Flagler", but he persuaded them to use the Indian name "Mayaimi". His intentions here were no different as he expected to capitalize on this achievement because Key West had the closest deep water port to Cuba, South America, and the soon to be constructed Panama Canal.

**Photo by BJBernreuter**

With the increase in population that was sure to follow the railroad, it was providential indeed that a larger Catholic Church was under construction. On January 29th, 1904, ground was broken for the new church and the foundations were begun on February 2nd, as indicated by the cornerstone inscription near the front doors of the Church.

**Brother C. Otten, SJ,**
Courtesy St. Charles Borromeo Church Collection.
Construction: St. Mary Star of the Sea collection (PD old)

The architect and builder was Brother Cornelius Otten, SJ. Originally from Holland, Brother Otten was instrumental in the design and construction of many Churches served by the Jesuits of the New Orleans Province throughout the southeast United States.

The expert economizing labor of Brother Otten reduced construction costs to $24,444.00. The stone blocks that went into its construction are poured concrete made from the oolitic limestone dug from the ground on which the Church stands and one of Brother Otten's "economizing" techniques was described in a letter dated August 16, 1946, from Henry B. Haskins to Colonel H. P. Baya:

"......The new church started in February 1904, is of concrete, made of limestone dug from the grounds, and beach sand. For use with such aggregate Father Friend instructed Brother Otten., S.J., to use a richer mixture of cement and had a box made for measuring cement. Brother Otten thought this was a waste of cement so (he) put a false bottom in it, and used this, until Father Friend found out and made him remove the false bottom."

In this same year of 1904, the Sisters of the Holy Names of Jesus and Mary were able to complete the enlargement of the Convent to nearly twice its original size by the addition of the northeast wing, at a cost of $22,000. The decorative steeple was erected on the addition to bring a balance in design between the old and the new. Considered the handsomest educational building in the State of Florida, it was truly a monument to the devotion and heroism of the good women who founded and maintained it.

St. Mary Sstar of the Sea Collection

**1905**      Finally completed, St. Mary Star of the Sea was the first non-wooden place of Catholic worship in South Florida. Although he never fully recovered from his illness, Father Friend still oversaw the completion of the church and it is to his judgments and financial astuteness that this magnificent church was erected for such a small sum.

**"As long as the church shall stand, it will be a monument to the earnest work and courageous zeal of the most devoted and beloved of pastors, Father Friend." Miami Metropolis, 1905**

St. Mary Star of the Sea was dedicated August 20th, 1905, by the Rt. Rev. William J. Kenny, D.D., Bishop of St. Augustine, accompanied by Father Friend, Rev. Snebelen, Rev. Latiolais, and Rev. Navin. At 9:30 AM the church grounds were already overflowing, as the procession marched around the church. The Bishop sprinkled holy water on the walls as he passed and upon returning to the entrance the doors were thrown open.

Bishop Kenny, DD

St. Mary Star of the Sea collection

The Bishop and entourage proceeded up the center aisle to the altar continuing with the blessing of the interior of the church. The congregation and guests followed, filling the church, choir loft, and aisles to capacity.

After the dedication ceremonies and before the solemnization of the Holy Mass, the Ayala's orchestra, accompanied by the grand organ, rendered selections from "Peter's Mass". Pastor Fr. Friend celebrated the High Mass at 10:30 assisted by Deacon Rev. Father Navin, Subdeacon Rev. Father Latiolais, and the altar boys. The Right Rev. Bishop Kenny read the sermon of Solomon, on the completion of the Temple in Jerusalem.

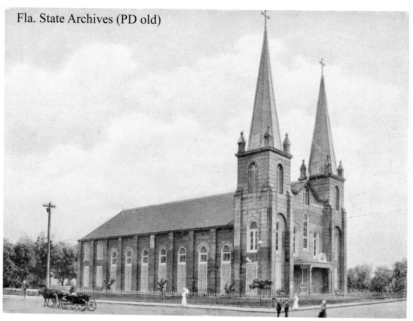

Fla. State Archives (PD old)

**"...and I have built this temple to honor the Lord, the God of Israel."**

1 Kings 8:20

Fr. Friend always intended to have a likeness of the recovered painting of St. Mary duplicated in stained glass as the centerpiece of the new church. However a shortfall in funds and an underestimation of the cost of this stained glass masterpiece required a substitute window similar in likeness to the side glass windows to be used. Not placated by the substitute for his envisioned stained glass window, he pursued his quest to have Our Lady Star of the Sea watch over her church, from a masterful work of glass and art above and behind the altar.

The Franz Mayer Company in Munich Germany, with offices in New York, was contracted to create the stain glass window of the Church Patroness. Known for their beautiful works in Europe, this German company reportedly had no experience with the effects of salt air on the lead and the staining of the glass to survive fading as a result of the tropical sun in the southern exposure.

(PD old)

Photo courtesy Franz Mayer Studio

Brother Cornelius Otten, S.J. researched the European firms that had built the magnificent windows prevalent in the Cuban capital of Havana, and working in collaboration with the New York office of the German company, they were able to learn the methods necessary to assure a beautiful and enduring image.

The German company required payment in full, in advance, with no terms. Father Friend shared the news with a group of parish men belonging to the newly formed Knights of Columbus Council 1015. This was Florida's sixth council, chartered May 8th of that same year with 36 charter members and F.C. Brossier serving as the first Grand Knight. The Knights agreed to raise the funds for the window.

The Key West populace, who had already nicknamed this beautiful structure "The Cathedral" because of its awe-inspiring spires, responded generously and the funds were reportedly collected

Photo by BJBernreuter

79

in two months' time.  The installation of the 3.9 meter (12 ft. 8 in.) high by 1.83 meter (6 ft.) wide stain glass window became the focal centerpiece of the Church and was celebrated in a city wide event with a second ceremony, reaffirming the first consecration, held on the Feast of the Immaculate Conception, December 8, 1907.  It was presided over by Rt. Rev. W. J. Kenny, D.D., Bishop of St. Augustine.

**1906**      The government house that sheltered the soldiers during the Spanish American War and used as the church for three years was saved and placed behind the newly remodeled Convent to be used as a kindergarten for children from 3 to 6 years old.

Chief Gunner C. Morgan, US Marines, presented the Sisters with copper plaques of the community seal of the Sisters of the Holy Names, which were attached to the iron gates.

State Archives of Florida, Florida Memory, http://floridamemory.com/show/36533 (PD old)

**1907**      On August 15, 1907, Father Friend celebrated his Sacerdotal Silver Jubilee.  Rev. Linus Schuler, SJ, was appointed the following September, to succeed Father Friend, who went to Miami, Florida.  The term of Father Schuler ended June 23, 1910, and Father Friend was re-appointed as pastor to take his place.

Although not as vigorous as in the past, Fr. Friend continued to take an active part in all parish work.  Continuously plagued by severe attacks of sickness, he was forced to retire on August 7, 1914.  Rev. O.M. Poche, SJ, replaced him that same day but because of poor health was also advised by physicians to leave.

During his last tenure as pastor Father Friend was assisted by Father Ina O'Shanahan in 1906, Father L.H. Stagg in 1908, and Father William J. Tyrell and Father James P. Moore in 1909.

In August of 1907 many of the sisters fell ill to dengue fever, including the Superior.

Work on the overseas railroad progressed and the population of Key West increased as more and more workers arrived. In 1909 two serious explosions occurred, one at Cudjoe Key and the other at Boca Chica. Many railway laborers were killed and injured. Our Catholic priests responded by hearing last confessions, anointing the wounded, and praying over the dead.

**1910**   Father P. Faget arrived to assist the growing parish in 1910, followed shortly by Father M.O. Semmes. The population had now increased to 19,945.

**1912**   January 22, 1912, is the day the train arrived. Once known as "Flagler's Folly" it now became "The Eighth Wonder of the World", the railroad that went to sea. Henry M. Flagler, 82 years old, stepped off his private car, the Rambler, and was greeted by the Mayor, Dr. Joseph N. Fogarty. Three days of celebration followed, but Flagler, old and tired, left Key West and went on to Havana, Cuba where he was quoted as saying, "Now I can die in peace," which he did a little over a year later.

Key West was now connected to the mainland of Florida and, as expected, a new era of tourism followed, swelling the population to 22,000. A person could ride the Florida East Coast Railway straight from New York to Key West.

There was one round trip each day, and on March 7, 1912, Cardinal Farley of New York honored this island parish with a day's visit as a guest of the Sisters of the Holy Names.

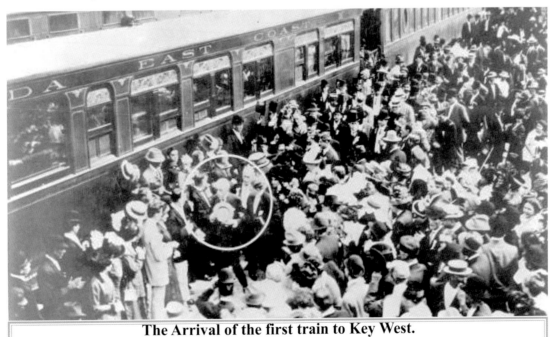

**The Arrival of the first train to Key West.**

**Henry M. Flagler is in the circle being escorted by Mayor Jeremiah Fogarty**
Courtesy of State Archives of Florida, Florida Memory, http://floridamemory.com/show/26695 (PD old)

**1913**     On May 19 of this year, Agustin Parla made the first solo flight from Key West to Mariel, Cuba.

**1915**     Sr. M. Caroline arrived in Key West from Tampa. She would eventually take charge of the Convent Museum and expand the exhibits considerably. She gathered fascinating specimens in formaldehyde, from an amoeba to a baby tiger. Most interesting were the shell, coins, and doll collections. The museum also included stuffed birds, snakes, butterflies, rocks & minerals, and artifacts from the USS *Maine*. (See picture on copyright page at beginning of book.)

**Sr. M. Caroline**
St. Mary Star of the
Sea collection

The Rev. J. Brislan, SJ, replaced Rev. O. Poche as pastor in 1915 with Father P. M. McDonnell and Father P. Redmond as his assistants. Church Diocesan records show that Father P.M. McDonnell became pastor on August 2, 1915 and was assisted by Father Theo de Beurme.

Fr. McDonald, realizing that the Chapel of <u>Nuestra Senora de la Caridad del Cobre</u> on Duval Street was no longer being used, had it removed and placed on the church's grounds. This became the first official parish residence. It later was used as a parish meeting hall and renamed St. Ann's Hall. (It is now the parish gift shop.)

Another long narrow building that had been erected during the war on the grounds of St. Joseph's School was also moved to the church property and later used as classrooms.

St. Mary Star of the Sea collection

Photo by BJBernreuter

**St. Ann's Hall before and now as the Parish Gift shop.**
**Standing on the porch are Violet Pita & Jo Petrick.**

# Chapter 8
## Wars-Prohibition-Depression

**1917**  The United States' entry into World War I transformed the island into a strategic Naval Port, living up to its moniker "The Gibraltar of the Gulf", given to it by Commodore David Porter in 1823. The world was changing; no longer storing warehouses of coal, it was oil, fuel, and diesel that the ships were in need of. The Navy now patrolled the shores with seaplanes, dirigibles, and surface ships, engaging German submarines and attempting to block enemy efforts to obtain oil from Mexican ports. During this era

**Thomas A. Edison at Key West Naval Station circa 1914-18**
State Archives of Florida, Florida Memory,

more than 500 sea plane pilots were trained here. Even the famous inventor Thomas A. Edison was brought here by the Navy to develop an anti-submarine device, the depth charge.

Although our sea-going craft had converted to oil based fuel, don't think such advancements had taken hold of our land forces. This was not yet the automotive age. Mule teams labored along dirt roads and the base commander's personal conveyance was a victoria carriage drawn by a spanking bay.

**Base Commander**
Monroe County Public Library  (pd old)

Shortly after the United States entered World War I in April 1917, the Knights of Columbus Supreme Knight James A. Flaherty (1909-1927) wrote President Woodrow Wilson a letter in which he reported that the Order proposed to "establish centers for the large body of men who will be concentrated in training and mobilization camps." These would be called "huts".

By that summer, the K of C War Activities Committee was established. The Knights established service centers in training camps; rest and recovery hostels in England and Ireland; "huts" behind the lines, and after the war, in allied occupied areas, under the banner "Everyone Welcome, Everything Free."

The Knights provided the servicemen with a wide range of social programs including sports, music and drama, while the K of C chaplains ministered to their spiritual needs. Following this directive, our local Knights of Columbus council built a social hall for service men that included a library, recreational equipment, an outside area for sports, and a stage. The hall fronted on Duval Street at the corner of Virginia, where the old Cuban chapel once stood; on the same stretch of land holding St. Joseph's School and St. Francis Xavier (today this is the entrance to Duval Square). The building was known in the parish as the N.C.C.S. Hall (National Catholic Community Service Hall). After the war it served as the public library.

**N.C.C.S. Hall as Public Library**
Monroe County Public Library (PD old 80)

**1918**      As the government did not always send chaplains to serve the military and their families stationed here, it fell to St. Mary Star of the Sea parish to care for their spiritual needs. Father McDonald therefore acted as an Auxiliary Chaplain for the Army and Navy during his term of office and was joined in 1918 by Father Lawrence T. Hanhauser. Although Rear Admiral Fletcher, Naval Base Commander, was not Catholic, he always attended Father McDonnell's Sunday Mass in the Naval Yard. Following Naval Regulations, the church pennant was always flown during Mass.

Up to this time the parochial house had been some crude sheds used by the Government for storing material during the Spanish American War. The new pastor, Father McDonald decided to upgrade the priest's living quarters. The new residence was begun April 30, 1917, but the turmoil of the Great War delayed

St. Mary Star of the Sea collection (PD scan)

its completion until May 3, 1918. It was of the same construction and material as the church and made tropically comfortable. To celebrate the opening of the new rectory, a distinguished gathering of military and city officials were on hand to honor the good work of our parish clergy.

**1919**       Having been approved by 36 states, the 18th Amendment (prohibition) was ratified on January 16, 1919 and became effective on January 16, 1920. It would last until 1933 and added another chapter to the colorful history of the island. With Cuba only 90 miles south, a new enterprise presented itself and "Rum-Runners" proliferated as a fast boat could make a round trip in one day.

On Aug. 6, 1919, Rev. L.P. White, SJ, was assigned as Pastor and Chaplain. He was assisted by Father A. L. Maureau, SJ. In addition to their regular ministries the priests were often called upon to bless the naval vessels in port and had such interesting duties as celebrating Mass aboard submarines.

On September 8, 1919, one of the worst storms up until that time ravished the island. The hurricane raged for 17 hours with such force that the government wind gauge broke while recording 98 miles an hour. Many of the old-timers here felt that the winds were considerably over 110 mph at times. More than 400 lives were lost due to this storm and the infrastructure of the city suffered severe damage as well.

The Catholic schools and the Church were badly damaged, and the Convent building was unroofed. The great storm damaged the San Carlos beyond repair and a delegation was sent to Havana to secure funds for its reconstruction.

**1920**     Henry Flagler's grand hotel, The Casa Marina, was completed on the south shores of the island. Planned by Flagler, construction started in 1918 but was delayed by the disastrous storm of the previous year. Three days after its grand opening, President Warren G. Harding came to visit, confirming its designation as a high-end destination resort.

### Catholic Daughters of the Americas

The Key West chapter of the Catholic Daughters of the Americas, Court #634, was formed April 24th of this year. This, the largest and oldest national organization of Catholic women in the world, was founded in 1903 by the Knights of Columbus in Utica, New York. It was originally called the "National Order of Daughters of Isabella and is dedicated to the principles of "Unity and Charity". In 1921 the name was changed to the Catholic Daughters of America (CDA) and they severed ties with the Knights of Columbus allowing it to become an independent organization.

There were 44 Charter Members: Leila Amador, Alifair Baldwin, Yvonne Baldwin, Mrs. Leo Boners, Clara and Dorothy Beaver (sisters of Fr. Beaver), Isabel Bernreuter, Cornelia Ball, Mrs. L. Bower, Rosalie DeBarce, Agnes, Mary, Lola, and May Carsteus, Margaret Dion, Virginia Demeritt, Amelia Fagan, Blanche Guiteres, Hortense A. Guiteres, Mrs. G. Guiteres, Ruby Jerguson, Alice Leon, Serafina Laza, Carrie Lester, Myrtle I. Lester, Helena M. Lester, Mary (Mamie) Moss, Virginia McCook, Mary Oliveros, Anna Percell, Josephine Piodela, Pauline Pinder, Sarah Roberts, Avelina Rios, Mamie Russell, Lenora Langyer, Julia Sands, Mrs. W. Sawyer, Eva M. Torano, Mary Vignol, Lorena Walton, Hesta C. Walton, Connie Wilson, Marion Uhrback, and Victoria Yardi. All of these good women were dedicated to strengthening their spiritual life through Christ and His Church.

Sister Mary Domina arrived in 1921, on the steamer *Concho*.

**1922**     On a bright sunny day May 25, 1922, the Feast of the Ascension, the stone grotto containing the statues of Our Lady of Lourdes and Saint Bernadette was dedicated. This was also the 25th anniversary of Sister Louis Gabriel's entrance into the religious profession of the Sisters of the Holy Names of Jesus and Mary. This artistic structure, made of natural rock gathered on school grounds, was designed by Sister Louis and made possible by the contributions from her many friends in the community.

Photo by BJBernreuter

Since her arrival in Key West, Sister Gabriel had experienced the severe destruction of three major storms: the October 11, 1909 hurricane, the October 17, 1910 hurricane and finally the September 12, 1919 storm that had just passed. Because of the devastation and heartache she had witnessed, she had a deep desire to keep Key West and its residents safe from future storms. From this arose her passion to build the grotto to seek protection from Our Blessed Mother Mary. Tradition tells us that Sister Louis Gabriel is said to have remarked that day, that as long as the grotto stood, "Key West would never experience the full brunt of a hurricane." And as all residents can attest, there has not been a severe storm on the island since the erection of the grotto in 1922.

**Sr. Louis Gabriel**
(PD scan)

**1923** From the archives of St. Augustine Diocese we learn that the enrollment of the Convent school was 520 white girls, the boys' school numbered 164 white boys, and the school for black children enrolled 158.

Active parochial organizations at this time were: Daughters of St. Ann, Catholic Daughters of America, Children of Mary for both white and black children, Boys' Sodality, Holy Angels, Infant Jesus, La Caridad del Cobre for the Cuban ladies, League of the Sacred Heart, and the Knights of Columbus.

**1924**  The San Carlos Institute was finally completed on October 10, five years after the previous building was destroyed in the hurricane of 1919. Noted for its ornate Spanish façade, it was designed by Francisco Centurión, one of Cuba's most prominent architects.

The pictures above display the parish and school properties from different angles. In the lower left hand corner of top photo, the street running diagonally from left to bottom center, is Duval St. The school property is outlined in blue. The dark roofed building at far left is the N.C.C.S. Hall. The next building is St. Francis Xavier, and then St. Joseph's on Simonton St. The lower photo shows the Convent of Mary Immaculate and St. Mary Star of the Sea both fronting Division St. One can also make out the new rectory, St. Ann's Hall next to it, and the government buildings. The very large building to the right is Gato's cigar factory.

**1925**    Rev. L. White, SJ, ended his tenure here August 26, 1925 and was replaced by Rev. P. Marnane, SJ, who served until January 9, 1931. He was joined in 1926 by Father J.E. Donohoe, and Father T.H. Bortellk in 1927, and William J. Harty in 1928, and finally by Father Michael F. Cronin in 1929. He was then replaced by the Rev. F. X. Dougherty, SJ, who was always in high spirits in spite of his poor health and served Key West until his death May 4, 1934.

**Rev. F.X. Dougherty**
BJBernreuter collection

**1927**    The first international air service was inaugurated by Pan American World Airways on October 28th, when a trimotor Fokker F-7 flew mail from Key West's Meacham Field to Havana, Cuba. Regular passenger service to Havana would begin the following year.

**1929**    The Great Depression was the longest and deepest depression of the 20th century. The Depression actually began with the fall in stock prices around September 4, 1929, and then with the stock market crash of October 29, known as Black Tuesday, it quickly spread to almost every country in the world. Key West took a free-fall from the richest city per capita in the nation to the poorest. Even with almost half of its population gone jobs were still scarce.

**1932**    This year extension courses in Education from Gainesville University were offered at the Convent of Mary Immaculate under the direction of Sister Catherine of the Blessed Sacrament, PhD, Fordham University.

**1934**    With more than 80% of Key West's population on relief there were rumors that Washington was planning to abandon the city and relocate the people elsewhere. A desperate plan was concocted by the city fathers and on July 1st, the city council along with the county commission surrendered the city charter to the state governor, David Sholtz. The Governor then declared "a state of emergency" existed in Key West and in turn handed the city over to Julius F. Stone Jr., the head of the Federal Emergency Relief Administration in Florida.

After careful scrutiny of the island's resources, it was decided that sunshine, warm weather, and beaches for relaxation would be the city's most enticing assets. "Tourism" - that was the future for Key West. A bit of a showman, Mr. Stone was able to capture free advertising by sending out dramatic press releases throughout the country.

Headlines all over the nation would read, "Surrender of Key West". Using Works Project Administration (WPA) writers and artists, he kept planting such stories over and over depicting the island as a tropical paradise.

The WPA then built hotels, beaches, and Key West's first attraction, the Key West Tropical Aquarium. The publicity worked, and Key West declared its first major tourist season a resounding success.

Yet the effects of the depression caused a severe loss of enrollment in the Catholic schools, forcing the boys' Jesuit high school to close permanently, after 18 years of operation by the Sisters on the Simonton Street property.

John Baldwin Jr., the son of John Baldwin whose estate sold the convent property to the nuns, worked for the Key West Fire Department. Due to the severity of the depression city employees were being paid in scrip and this was being discounted at grocery stores for as little as 25 cents on the dollar. In consideration of his family's plight, the Sisters allowed him and his family to occupy a one story frame dwelling on the Convent grounds. In exchange for this free rent, John would milk the cows and perform various handy jobs for the nuns. This he did until he became too old. He continued to live on the grounds until a few months before his death at 91 years of age in 1953.

Another casualty of the depression was Council 1015 of the Knights of Columbus, which dissolved after faithfully serving the parish for 29 years.

The Rev. William Reagan, SJ, replaced Fr. Dougherty and served from June 5, 1934 until August 4, 1938. Assisting Father Reagan during his tenure was, Father James J. O'Brien arriving in 1935, Father L.M. O'Neill in 1936, and finally Father Raymond Jerome Mullin who assisted in 1937.

The fall of this year saw the arrival of Reverend Semmes, SJ, (cousin of Sister Catherine Semmes), who was appointed by his provincial to found a mission for the Colored of Key West. After combing the city in vain to find a suitable building in which to begin his work, Father finally decided to use a large classroom, which was connected with St. Francis Xavier's school, as a chapel. On September 9th the first Mass was celebrated there and attended by more than one hundred parishioners. A new apostolic venture had been launched.

At first the mission was not accepted well by the black congregation as they felt that they had been put out of St. Mary Star of the Sea Parish. This was understandable since Jim Crowism was rampant at this time. Eventually though, they began to appreciate that for the first time they would be able to participate fully in the life of a parish. As members of St. Mary's they were denied membership in the usual parish organizations, such as altar boys and adult choir.

Less than a year after the opening of the new mission Father Semmes was reassigned to another parish and Father A. L. Mareau, SJ, was only able to celebrate Mass at the chapel on Sundays and Holy days. The black congregation organized sales, bazaars, plays, anything they could to raise money to build a new church. They formed a fund raising group called "St. Francis Xavier's Willing Workers", to raise money. Many gifts, donations, and church articles arrived from families of the Sisters, from St. Peter Claver (the Colored Mission in Tampa), the Holy Name Sisters in New York and in Tampa, and the Ursuline Sisters in New Orleans. Despite all this support and an increase in parishioners, the chapel and mission was disbanded in 1941.

The Lord is wondrous, and at times we may not understand His ways, but in time He always reveals Himself. It would seem that it was not His plan for His people to be divided. The Church recognized that everyone should fully participate in the Mass, but not separately. Full integration would take time, but this began the process. St. Mary Star of the Sea is so much richer in love, spirit, and understanding today because of this unity.

**1935** (Matecumbe, a name that may be corrupted from Spanish "mata hombre" translated "kill man".) On Labor Day, September 2, 1935, in the Matecumbe Keys the barometer was rapidly dropping to a low of 26.35… the lowest reading ever recorded in this hemisphere. The most powerful storm ever to make landfall in the U.S. was about to strike. Forever after known as the Labor Day Hurricane of 1935 this 200 plus mile an hour Category 5 hurricane totaled more than six million dollars in damages. The total loss of life is unknown but more than 600 bodies were recovered.

Under the protection of Our Lady of Lourdes, Key West remained unscathed by this monstrous storm, however no one remained emotionally untouched by the devastation of the upper Keys and the loss of family and friends throughout Monroe County. Our priests were attending to the burials, consolation, and mental havoc heaped on a community now struggling to provide assistance to the few remaining camps and villages of the upper Keys. Many of the survivors were brought and sheltered here in Key West; but due to the humidity and heat, lack of transport, and the constant discovery of more bodies, many of the dead had to be burned in funeral pyres.

The Overseas Railroad was dead and Key West was once again isolated from the mainland. But every dark cloud has a silver lining and from the wreckage of the railroad emerged the beginnings of the Overseas Highway.

**1938**    Long before the hurricane destroyed the railway, it was already in receivership. Had Flagler still been alive, he probably would have rebuilt it; however the company decided to abandon the overseas extension and transferred its car ferries to Port Everglades.

The Monroe County Toll Bridge Commission purchased the railroad right of way for $3,600,000, through a loan from the Public Works Administration. At first car ferries were used to connect several of the stretches still over open water, but as the bridges were gradually completed these were eliminated. On March 29, the longest overseas highway in the world opened for traffic and Key West was once again connected, at least physically, to the mainland. July 4th was the official opening date and the tourists returned, this time in buses and their own automobiles.

This year the Convent celebrated its 70th anniversary and the Rev. Patrick J. Kelleher, SJ, was assigned to St. Mary's to replace Rev. Reagan.

**Pres. Franklin D. Roosevelt**
Monroe County Public Library (PD scan)

**1939**    The rumbling of distant drums could be heard from across the Atlantic, and February 18th saw the arrival of President Franklin D. Roosevelt, who travelled by car over the new "Overseas Highway" to Key West to observe war games in the Caribbean. Key West mayor, Willard Albury, met the president at the west end of the Bahia Honda bridge and from there accompanied the president to the Key West naval facilities. The president then met with the Chief of Naval Operations, Admiral Leahy, aboard the USS *Houston*. This inspection preceded the reopening of the Naval Station on November 1, 1939, two years before the U.S. entry into World War II.

Key West honored President Roosevelt with a parade unequaled since the arrival of Flagler. To acknowledge all the benefits received through his Federal Emergency Relief Program, the Works Progress Administration (WPA), and the Public Works Administration the beautiful boulevard which surrounds most of the island's water front was named in his honor.

**1940**    Father John J. Murphy arrived to assist Rev. Patrick Kelleher. This year Fr. Kelleher was required to complete WPA Form 20, a Historical Records Survey from 1939. The interesting information on the form is in answer to question 9 where Father Patrick lists the year of the church's organization as *1840*, with no

dates of lapse or being defunct. He mentions the Mass held in City Hall in 1846, referencing it as a building used as the church. His further answers on the next page show some confusion as to what the survey is trying to ascertain. Is it the "church" or the "present building" that is of interest? Not knowing what his sources or intentions were there are no conclusions to be

Fr. Patrick J. Kelleher, SJ
St. Mary Star of the Sea collection

drawn by these remarks. They are just interesting historical documents. This form is shown in the back of this history as Exhibits A and B on pages 180 & 181.

The ravages of time, tropical weather, and termites caused so much damage to the wooden structures of the church that Father Kelleher decided to make repairs and improvements to the interior of the church. To raise funds, Father Kelleher held a nine day "Benefit Frolic" at La Concha Park. He had a program printed which summarized the history of the parish up until that time. His opening letter in the program was beautifully written and deserves attention here.

Photos courtesy of St. Mary Star of the Sea collection

This photo depicts the original wooden altar, communion railing and facade behind the altar. Note the ornate woodwork of the side altar. This gives you an idea of the craftsmanship and beauty of the main altar. Details of this altar are more apparent in the close up above, and in the picture on the next page. The St. Joseph statue appears to be the same one from the original church. Also note the absence of any electric lighting.

**Detail of original sanctuary with wooden communion rails**
St. Mary Star of the Sea collection

Father Kelleher writes: *"On this coral isle, the southernmost city of our beloved country, lifting her stately spires heavenward, greeting the weary gaze of traveler by sea and land, stands the church of St. Mary Star of the Sea. Her Gothic structure dedicated to God's glory has brought spiritual consolation to visitor and resident alike. Her Glorious Patroness, Mary Star of the Sea, has guided for nearly a century many a mariner over life's troubled sea."*

He engaged the services of the Panzironi Company, church decorators of New York. During the renovation and repairs, an Italian marble altar was donated and replaced the elaborate wooden structure. The altar consists of seven types of marble and served as the altar of sacrifice. Below the tabernacle on the altar of repose is a marble and gold leaf mosaic of the Chi-Rho cross flanked by the alpha and omega. The four marble columns and their capitals on the front ends of this altar repeat the Romanesque style of the columns and capitals originally constructed in the nave of the Church.

This altar is attached to the floor and is considered a fixed altar. Therefore it was dedicated and, according to church traditions, had the relic of a martyr or saint placed under the altar. The General Instruction of the Roman Missal, No. 302, contains the following statement: "The practice of placing relics of Saints, even those not Martyrs, under the altar to be dedicated is fittingly retained. Care should be taken, however, to ensure the authenticity of such relics."

[**AUTHOR'S NOTE:** The previous altar of St. Mary's was wood and therefore may not have had a relic placed under it. If it did, then that same relic may have been transferred to this new altar. This marble altar has a small repository, about two by four inches and approximately an inch and a half deep in the center of the altar table and directly in front of the tabernacle. It is not known what or whose relic was placed in this altar and that may not be that uncommon.]

A tabernacle, also of Carrara Marble, with an inlaid decorative mosaic in the cap was procured and securely fixed on the altar. The front brass tabernacle door depicts in relief the Annunciation of the Archangel Gabriel to the Blessed Virgin Mary with the presence of the Holy Spirit and the inscription: ET VERBVM CARO FACTIVM EST (THE WORD WAS MADE FLESH) — John 1:14.

Iron communion rails, electric chandeliers, and sanctuary chairs were added as well as a tester above the altar from which hung drapes as a background for a large crucifix. The crucifix, with a masterly carved corpus, was suspended above the tabernacle and below the stained glass. As shown in the photo at left the side altars were changed also. There is the heart shaped candle holder and note the large fan. Fans were also in the sanctuary as this was before air-conditioning.

**1941**     Father Kelleher's term on our island came to an end in July of 1941, as he was appointed pastor to Saint Ann's church in West Palm Beach. A new pastor, Rev. Thomas Atherton, SJ, arrived assisted by Father Terrence King and later by Father White.

**1942**     The following was written by Fr. Atherton to honor the ninetieth anniversary of St. Mary, Star of the Sea:

*"Through ninety years "star-gazers" have come down here to the sea, Men who "have seen a Star" . . . "Have come to adore Him" and to make Him adored. They have known their human frailty and weakness. As Mary had been God's instrument through which the True Light radiated into the world which sat in darkness and the shadow of death, as this Blessed Virgin had been the inspiration of the Apostles, as she had gone before all Christianizing endeavor . . . so she has been the Star steering the course for the mariners of God and shining the Divine Light upon this ... the Southernmost Key of the Land of the Stars and Stripes. AVE, MARIS STELLA! HAIL, THOU STAR OF THE SEA!"*

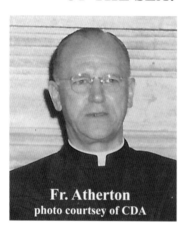

**Fr. Atherton**
**photo courtsey of CDA**

This prose, written at the onset of America entering the war, speaks of a world sitting in darkness under the shadow of death, but through the guidance of Mary, Bearer of the Divine Light, her priests, the mariners of God, have been drawn to this island to bring His Light among us.

And, out of evil, God can make good things happen. So it was on September 22, of 1942, that water from Florida City, on the mainland, flowed for the first time in Key West, through a pipeline built by the Navy to support the massive troop buildup that was occurring.

The Knight's hall was vacated by the public library to serve once again as the local U.S.O. operating under the auspices of N.C.C.S. as a recreation center for our sailors and soldiers. Many dances and parties for our military men were held here on weekends providing a place for them to socialize.

After the war it continued as a U.S.O., as well as serving as the parish hall for meetings, bazaars, parish dinners, and bingo throughout the years. It was undoubtedly the center of our parish social life and utilized by all ministries of St. Mary Star of the Sea.

In 1943 Fr. Atherton was joined by Father Joseph H. Johnson, SJ, who replaced him as Pastor in 1945. Rev. Johnson was assisted by Father Frank Kness and Father M.O. Semmes, who had returned. Father John McHugh and Father John Jacob Capelle joined the parish as assistants in 1946.

**St. Mary Star of the Sea 1950's**
Monroe County Public Library Original byPhoto Lewis McLane (BJB scan)

# Chapter 9
## One Hundred Years

**1948**        Rev. Joseph Maring, SJ, arrived as pastor in 1948 and had Father Michael J. Cronin, SJ, as his assistant. This was Father Mike's fiftieth year as a priest.

Father Joseph F. Beaver was the first Key West native to be ordained as a Jesuit, at St. Mary's College in Kansas, and may even have been the first to be ordained as a priest.

Sr. Louis Gabriel died peacefully on September 13, 1948 a good and faithful servant to the Lord and her community. Monsignor William Barry of St. Patrick's in Miami gave her eulogy stating among other honors and praises that she had served as a "lamp of faith" to this community for fifty one years. She was buried in the nuns' cemetery on the convent grounds. The graduating class of CMI dedicated their yearbook Stella Maris, to the good sister with these words, ***"Through the devotion shown during the entire fifty-one years of her religious life to the pupils of C.M.I., and because, in her sweet and cheerful way, she is always ready to render her services to all, Sister M. Louise Gabriel has won a place in the heart of every student."***

**1949**        1949 marked the Golden Anniversary of the Jesuit Fathers of the New Orleans Province who had been serving in Key West since 1898.

**Auditorium with boarder's residence on 2nd floor.**

The blessing of the new auditorium with the boarders' residence on the second floor occurred in April of 1949. At a cost of $105,000, this grand building had a seating capacity of 600.

This year the good priests of Key West established a mission up the Keys for the 30 to 40 Catholics living in a settlement called Marathon. This mission continued until the parish of San Pablo was formed in 1956.

Although many of the statues have been replaced through the various restorations beginning in the 1940s, they carefully reflect the devotional faith of the people. One elder parishioner explained the statues surrounding the baptismal font: the Sacred Heart of Jesus, the crowned Our Lady of Mt. Carmel with the infant Jesus, and the Infant of Prague are about God's love. The statues on the other side: Saint Joseph, Saint Anthony and La Virgin de la Caridad de Cobre, the patroness of Cuba, are about those who loved as God commanded.

The individual offering of the statues indicate the vitality of the devotional faith of the people. An example is the Infant of Prague. During World War II, there was great devotion to this image among mothers of soldiers deployed in the war. One such mother, Mrs. Ursalina Toppino had three sons deployed in combat simultaneously. In her anxiety, she invoked the help of the Infant of Prague for her children. Upon their safe return to their home, she offered the image of the Infant of Prague to the Church in gratitude and for the benefit of all who invoke His help.

Mother Mary Gustave, Sup. Gen.
St. Mary Star of the Sea collection

In 1949 Father Gabinus Egana also came to assist Father Maring. Later that year, Father Curtis Washington, the first black priest ordained in Florida, celebrated Mass at St. Mary's. He was on his way to work in the missions of Africa. In 1951 they were joined by Father Charles Roccaforete and Father Michael Watters.

That November the convent was honored with a visit from Mother Mary Gustave, Superior General of the Sisters of the Holy Names. A grand reception was held for her in the new auditorium.

**1952**     Father John J. Capelle returned to Key West in 1952.

On February 26, 1952, St. Mary Star of the Sea parish celebrated its one hundredth anniversary since the dedication of the first church and its resident pastor. Father Maring organized this special event with a week long spiritual and joyful celebration. The Most Reverend Thomas J. McDonough, DD (Doctor of Divinity), Auxiliary Bishop of St. Augustine, began the scheduled ceremonies early in the week with a solemn high Mass for the clergy and the children. The celebrations continued with carnivals and festivities, culminating with a rare and impressive Solemn Pontifical High Mass which was sung by the Most Reverend Francis E. Hyland, DD. Thanks to Mr. John Spottswood, this Holy Mass was carried live on the airways from the church sanctuary, by his Radio Station WKWF, Key West, Florida.

*"Sanctify the fiftieth year" Almighty God commanded His people through His servant Moses. Each fiftieth year must be a year of special jubilee - of joyful gratitude, merciful pardon, determined Amendment – twice 50 years we have had a Jubilee of this church in this southernmost island city."*

**Father Maring 1952**

Fr. Joseph Maring, SJ
photo courtsey of CDA

## Knights of Columbus Council 3652

It is probably not coincidental that during this historical anniversary year the parish men would band together and reestablish the Knights of Columbus presence in Key West by forming the Frances X. Doughtery Council 3652.

The following men formed the charter council under their Grand Knight, R.P. Eepoel: G.P. Bonamy, E.B. Buckley, L.I. Disirito, H.E. Duncan, L.L. Eisner, P.J. Erickson, E.J. Lauriha, M.I. Lester, D.E. McCurdy, F.B. Piodela, R.H. Ray, L.A. Rockoff, J.M. Stewart, L.M.J. Eisneer, A.T. Warnock, J.C. Betancourt, D.A. Yaccarino, A.V. Martinez, J.B. Anderson, J.Tallon, P.A. Toppino, A.J.Fricke, F.X. Delaney, J.A. Hull, R.A. Howard, J.F. Coen, J.W. Fiedeldey Jr., G.R. Koch, Rev. J. Maring, S.J., H.J. Crean, S.M. Whalton, W.H. Adams, V.S. Davis, E. Martinez, J.P. Lenihan, C.S. Kraeger, J.W. Schnatterer, J.F. Del Villar, V.E. Stine, E. Toppino, F.P. Toppino, H.C.J. Eisner, A. Lopez, Jr., L. Fradette, J.G. Cronk, and R.J. Gugliemo.

In 1952 the Convent of Mary Immaculate was renamed Mary Immaculate High School because the school became coeducational as seven boys were admitted to the freshman class. This first coed class would graduate in 1956.

St. Joseph's School
Monroe County Public Library

Sr. Mary Domina
St. Mary Star of the Sea
collection

## St. Joseph's School 1952-1960 My Memories

1952 is the year I began first grade at St. Joseph's School; my teacher was Sister Cecilia Rose, (Sr. Audrey Rowe, SNJM), a very beautiful nun who was undertaking her first assignment. Of course I fell in love with her. The principal was Sr. M. Frederick Joseph. My second grade teacher was Mrs. C.V., at least that's what she had us call her, and the principal was Sr. Olive Denise. In grade three my teacher was Mrs. Santini, and classes were in the new portable building. In 1955, Sr. Marguerite De-Louvain (Maris L'Ecuyer) was my fourth

Photo by BJBernreuter

**Mrs. Santini, 3rd. Grade**

grade teacher. She retired in 1957. She was very short, under five feet, slender but not fragile. She was a disciplinarian and maintained order with a heavy 18 inch ruler, as my knuckles bear testimony to. But she was good for us and you can be sure that teaching forty-one fourth grade boys in a hot classroom was not an easy chore. Through some good advice from my mother, I would stay after school and help her clean up the classroom. We became great friends, and I became a better student. I could now see behind the scenes and developed a deep respect for the Sisters of the Holy Names of Jesus and Mary. Sr. Eustelle-Marie was principal that year, but a year later Sr. M. John became principal until 1959.

I must have slept through fifth grade because I don't remember much about it at all, but my report card has Mrs. R. M. Husty as my teacher. Sixth grade was terrible, Mr. Egan was our teacher, he had a bad temper and would throw chalk at me to get my attention. Sr. Mary Domina, was my seventh grade teacher at St. Joseph's. She was another strong willed disciplinarian. If you were naughty, you were punished, but always you were loved. A nun can really give good hugs.

Sr. Eustelle-Marie returned as principal and my teacher for eighth grade. She made us aware that we were no longer children, but young adults. I graduated from the eighth grade, St. Joseph's School class of 1959-1960, which was the last graduating class from that school.

**St. Joseph's Altar boys 1958**
St. Mary Star of the Sea collection

That summer after graduating, my brother John and I, and a few others helped to demolish the old St. Joseph's School building. You might think this would be a student's dream, to tear down his school; although we made jokes and laughed about it, there was a disquieting feeling that a real loss was taking place. Sights and sounds that would never be experienced by another boy. Eight years of joy, tears, fights, friendships, learning, and in fact most of my life up until then had been spent at St. Joseph's School.

I would like to comment on "the fence". I'm not at all sure what discrimination was like in the beginning, when the schools were erected in the 1880s, but St. Joseph's and St. Francis's playgrounds were separated by a chicken-wire fence when I was attending. At recess, as the children played, sometimes a ball would go across that gulf and be politely returned to the other side, but the fence never came down and no one ever crossed from one side to the other.

Not much real communication occurred between the races that I was aware of. There was no animosity, no fear… we were just on the other side of the fence from each other, that's the way it was. This was the culture in which we were raised. Nobody talked about it. Our teachers never talked about it, and sadly, none of us asked. There was no understanding it; like the ocean, the trees, the sidewalks, the water fountains at Kress, and … the fence, it was just there.

Things of this nature were only whispered about by great aunts and great grandmothers. Nothing explained… nothing asked… and nothing answered. How sad that it took so long.

Bob J. Bernreuter

No one person can accurately relate the times, places, and people of an era. Every thought is a reflection of their education, environment, and culture. Understanding this, I have used many resources in the gathering of information for this history. In that vein I now offer these reflections from various students of St. Francis Xavier who can relate that experience in their own words.

**St. Francis Xavier Contradictory Fence 1938 – 1945**

I attended St. Francis Xavier from first grade to eighth grade. My father Joseph Welters all of my uncles and my sister Barbara Welters Mingo graduated from St. Francis also. We had Sr. Caroline, Sr. Lawrence Marie, and Mrs. Crimmins as teachers. Raymond Casamayor and Robert Whyms were some of my classmates. We didn't have a problem with the fence because we would push it down during recess and the boys from both St. Joseph and St. Francis would play baseball or basketball in the yard behind the school. When the bell rang we would put the fence back up. The sisters didn't admonish us at all.

Ralph Welters

**St. Francis Xavier School**
Monroe County Public Library

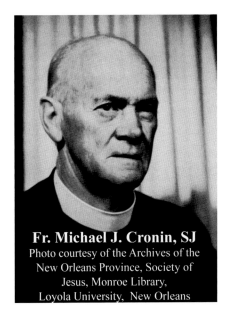

**Fr. Michael J. Cronin, SJ**
Photo courtesy of the Archives of the
New Orleans Province, Society of
Jesus, Monroe Library,
Loyola University, New Orleans

### In my own words!

I had decided a long time ago, after removing the last rock from beneath St. Francis Xavier School, that life is like a bowl of cherries... The rocks were removed by orders of Sister Hilda Rose and Father Cronin. So you will get a picture of what I am referring to, several of the students at St. Francis were asked to go under the school building and remove the loose rocks that were found. I was one of the chosen! Was this a form of discipline (I needed it), or did the rocks need to be removed? I do not remember if this incident occurred before I had a coconut thrown at me by Sister Hilda Rose or was it after? I often think about the good times I had at St. Francis, but the aforementioned incidents would not have happened in today's climate of teacher/student relationship.

Perhaps the discipline at St. Francis lends itself to the original setup of the school. Our school, St. Francis, was separated by a chicken wire fence, from St. Joseph's. St. Francis was an all-black, co-ed elementary from first grade to the eighth grade. St. Joseph's was an all-white, male elementary school. A chicken wire fence literally separated the two schools. There was a nice, beautiful skirt around the building at St. Joseph's, so rock digging beneath the building would not have been necessary. How about the tossing of coconuts at their students? They probably did not allow coconuts on the campus.

The highlight of my memories at St. Francis is: despite the chicken wire fence and the state laws that promoted segregation, we played and mixed together as if the laws or segregation did not exist on our beautiful island. I often thank God for allowing me to be one of the fortunate people to have been born, raised, and educated in Key West. Life was just a bowl of cherries while growing up in Key West and attending St. Francis Xavier!

Alvin Mitchell Leggett

## St. Francis Xavier 1953 – 1961

St. Francis was a Black, Coed, Parochial school operated by the Nuns of Mary Immaculate Star of the Sea Convent in Key West. The girls wore maroon skirts, beanies for the head, white blouses and "loafers" shoes. The boys wore brown khaki pants and white shirts.

All six of my siblings and I attended St. Francis Xavier School for our Elementary and Middle School education. When I graduated in the 8th grade, my parents wanted to transfer me to St. Mary's Immaculate School, which was an "All White Girls School." Since integration was not prevalent at the time, my parents were told by Sister Superior that I had to be a Roman Catholic in order to attend St. Mary's School. My religious denomination is "Episcopalian." Therefore, I had to attend Public School for the next four years until I graduated even though my parents would have like my siblings and I to have twelve years at the parochial schools.

I had great memories of the numerous Nuns, Fr. Cronin, and the lay teachers that taught me during my tenure at St. Francis Xavier. I was particularly fond of Sister Samuel and Fr. Cronin. I did not feel that way about Sr. Hilda Rose, for she seemed to favor the Catholic students more.

Our Annual Picnic was very special. Fr. Cronin sponsored our picnic to Sugarloaf Key. On the bus, we sang songs going and songs coming back. I remember the special song that we always sang to Fr. Cronin coming back home

from the picnic , "Oh we thank you Fr. Cronin yes we do, Oh we thank you Fr. Cronin yes we do, oh we had a lot of fun and we are  sorry it is done, oh we thank you Fr. Cronin yes we do."

I had so many wonderful  and bittersweet memories  during  the eight years that I spent at St. Francis, and these memories will live on in me forever.

Marcia Sweeting-Somersall

### St. Francis Xavier 1954 - 1961

I attended St. Francis Xavier elementary school from first grade in 1953 to my graduation from eighth grade in 1961.  I am an African American female who is Roman Catholic.  St. Francis Xavier was the only Roman Catholic coed school for African Americans at that time and was run by The Sisters of the Holy Names of Jesus and Mary.  I have very fond memories of grades one through six. I had Sr. Cecilia Ann, my Godmother Mrs. Leoncie Graham Crimmins, Sr. Samuel and my cousin Mrs. Barbara Welters Mingo as teachers.  All of my father's family were graduates of St. Francis Xavier.  They were all positive role models.  There was never favoritism or prejudice in any of those classes.  I know this because I experienced my first encounter with racism at the age of three years old in South Carolina.  Every summer I visited relatives in Miami, Georgia or New York and had to adjust my actions according to the contradictions that I encountered.

Upon returning to Key West I was safe except Kress (the water fountains) the skating rink, the bowling alley, and the fence between St. Joseph's and St. Francis Xavier.  We were told how much Jesus loved everyone but we couldn't cross the fence (a contradiction).  I had music lessons with Sr. Elizabeth, no problem, unless I didn't know my piano and violin lessons. She treated everyone, Black and White, the same.  She walked the talk.  All of her students participated in concerts and plays together (a contradiction).

Seventh and eighth grades were different.  I had Sr. Hilda Rose.  The fence issue, her treatment of the non-Roman Catholics, and the children with darker skin, created the uncharitable sin of indifference in me towards her.  I had it honed to a science until I attended St. Francis de Sales Catholic High School which was founded by St. Katherine Drexel in Powhatan, VA.  All of the nuns (Sisters of the Blessed Sacrament) there, walked the talk.

I wouldn't trade growing up here in Key West for anything because the memorable experiences and THE CONTRADICTIONS, helped me navigate through the different states (Virginia, Alaska, Texas, Georgia, New York and New Jersey) that I have lived in and life.

Ursula Welters Elliott

# Reflections on St. Francis Xavier

Reflecting upon my childhood in Key West, Florida often leads me to the markedly varied experiences I had in grade school at St. Francis Xavier Catholic school for African American/Black (AA/B) children and adolescents. Interestingly, many of the AA/B children in Key West attended either of two kindergarten programs prior to going to first grade. Those programs were that of Ellen Welters Sanchez (a relative of mine who was an accomplished musician, play-write, and seamstress; a descendant of the Welters brothers who generated and maintained the famed Welters Cornet Band. They were all Catholics) and Ms. Nora (I don't remember her last name) who was a devote Episcopalian.

Ms. Nora's school was directly affiliated with St. Peter's Episcopalian church in Key West, which in my understanding was seen as the Black Episcopalian church.

Once I embarked upon first grade at St. Francis, it was CLEAR that we, the AA/B students of St. Francis were somehow different than the students at St. Joseph's school (the school for white and Hispanic boys, directly next to St. Francis) and St. Mary Immaculate school (the school for white and Hispanic girls, near St. Mary Star of the Sea Church). While there were times all of the schools, including St. Francis, would attend a gathering in the auditorium near St. Mary Immaculate school, most of our educational and extracurricular activities were separate and hopefully equal.

As I think about those years now, I realize that we, the AA/B children were essentially viewed as a part of the mission work of the St. Mary Star of the Sea Parish. I can remember a statement made by the principal of St. Francis, a rather robust Canadian, who seemed to be very proud of her service to the AA/B children and their families, but was not hesitant to talk about her mission to "these" people. I am going to paraphrase now, but I remember her statement to entail most of the following: "We are proud to serve you little chocolate bunnies." This statement came after a series of gifts had been shared with us from a province in Canada.

Statements of this type were common, but this one has been ever present with me for about fifty years. This memory along with the reflection that there were no Black nuns and only two Black teachers, Barbara Mingo and Wilhelmina Bastian, throughout my years at St. Francis keeps me aware of the racism of that time. And, it was sad that the Catholic school for AA/B children and adolescents went only to the eighth grade, noting the limited expectations for higher education for this population by the Catholic Church. An eighth grade education for Blacks was the standard in this particular Catholic community for many years.

106

Another interesting memory that comes up for me from time-to-time has to do with the annual picnics we experienced, notably subsidized by the priests of St. Mary Star of the Sea Church. I can remember in particular Father Cronin, who was very connected with the Black community in Key West. In addition to sponsoring and participating in the annual end -of -the -year picnics at Sugar Loaf Key, he made frequent (sometimes unannounced) visits to the homes of many Black Catholics. He visited my grandmother (Anna Welters) and a family friend (Ms. Minnie Gandolfo) often and he would give us, the children a present, a dime or quarter for ice cream or a coke. Father Cronin seemed to be a very sincere man, but in my adult eyes there was a lot of paternalistic gestures to the extent that I cringe now as I think about how childlike many adult Black people behaved in his presence. I have dreams from time-to-time of singing our closing song to the annual picnics, "We thank you Father Cronin, yes we do. We thank you Father Cronin, yes we do!" I am not sure why the memory of that song bothers me, but it does!!!

It is important to note that we did in fact receive a good education at St. Francis Xavier. High level performance was an expectation along with religious diligence. I had to smile when the movie the "Passion" premiered, because as Catholic children we had been steeped in the passion of Christ and totally aware of the awfulness of that experience. We had via daily catechism studies learned in great detail the utter burden of the plight of Jesus the Christ.

Though we were separated in our educational processes we were included in the developmental milestones of Catholicism, namely first communion and Confirmation. At those ceremonies we, the AA/B candidates, were allowed to sit with the other (white/Hispanic) children, but our ordinary place was at the back of the church. In truth, the back of the church was the place for Black Catholics until the early 1960s. The actual date of the shift I cannot recall, but it was about the time that the schools were integrated. I can remember that my cousin, Adrian Welters, attended the "white" Catholic high school and he was five years my junior.

There are so many things to remember about St. Francis Xavier, but one of my favorite memories is reading outside with my classmates under the tutelage of one teacher or another in the early afternoon. It was during moments like that when my teachers reinforced our talents and shaped us fervently in the direction of excellence that I am pleased to have had the St. Francis experience despite the level of racism that prevailed.

Juliette Martin-Thomas

I can't thank these dear souls enough for sharing their memories. I know it broadened my perspective to see the view from the other side of the fence. It is humbling. I have one more to share and if you are like me you will find it very moving and a good life lesson for all the students that day...

### The Lunch

My name is DeChantal Milian Williams, I attended St France Xavier from first grade until eighth. I went to Douglas for one year then I went to high school at Mary Immaculate High School. The only discrimination I encountered was on a high school field trip. We were returning to Key West when the Catholic school bus stopped at Stuckey's Restaurant on the Keys for lunch. The Nuns and all my classmates got off and went in. We sat down and the waitress said that myself and Marlene Chipchase had to leave because they did not serve US. The Nun told us to go get back on the bus. The other students were then told to order the most expensive items on the menu. They all did, after all the orders were made, the Nun told them to get back on the bus without eating or paying for anything. Those classmates and I are still very much friends to this day.

DeChantal Milian Williams

**1953**     Father G. B. Hamilton arrived to assist Father Maring in 1953 followed by Father J. McEnaney and Father Anton Kness as assistants in 1954. A new school building is added to St. Joseph's School, to contain the third and fourth grades.

**1955**      In 1955 Father J. F. Curtin arrived to help the parish; he took over leadership of the St. John Bercham Altar Boy Society, training us in Latin and certifying us to serve. I was one of his students and will always remember those days behind the church, sitting on the cistern, reciting our Latin responses under his tutelage. None of us will forget the initiation rites up the Keys conducted by the older altar servers. Seaweed is itchy stuff! But it was a good time, good memories, and blessings have rained down upon us all.

This year saw students from St. Francis Xavier and St. Joseph's School practice band together for games played with Douglass High School (Key West's high school for black children), leading one Sister to remark, "Non-segregation does not bother these young men."

Segregation is not natural as the lyrics of the song "You've Got to be Taught", from the musical South Pacific, teaches us:

**You've got to be taught... to be Afraid**
**Of people whose eyes... are oddly made**
**And people whose skin... is a different shade**
**You've got to be carefully taught.**

**1956**      In August of 1956 the Rev. Father Joseph Beaver, SJ, a native Key Wester, returned to Key West as Pastor of St. Mary's. Born in Key West in 1918, Fr. Beaver had attended St. Joseph's School for boys. He later moved to Mobile, Alabama and graduated from Spring Hill High School. He entered the Society of Jesus at Grand Coteau, La., in 1935, then attended Spring Hill College in Alabama, and was ordained in 1948. He taught at Loyola University in New Orleans before coming to Key West.

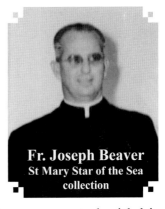

**Fr. Joseph Beaver**
**St Mary Star of the Sea collection**

A very smart man, who got things done, Fr. Beaver quickly reconnected with his many friends in the parish and established goals. He was assisted in 1957 by Father Rodney Kissinger and in 1958 by Father Michael Cutcliff.

MIHS had its first coed graduating class in 1956.

**1958**      The rapid growth of South Florida since the 1940s overtaxed the abilities of the Diocese of St. Augustine resulting in the creation of a new diocese comprising the 16 counties of South Florida. In 1958, Bishop Coleman F. Carroll, was installed as the first Ordinary of the new Diocese of Miami. He came from a family of three priest brothers: Bishop Howard Carroll of the Altoona-Johnstown Diocese, and Monsignor Walter Carroll who was serving in the Vatican Secretariat with Cardinal Montini (Pope Paul VI).

**This is the Star of the Sea Band which was formed around 1957-58 with students from CMI, MIHS, and St. Joseph's school.**

1st Row L to R: Gary Pantaleo, Frank Madiedo, _____, Lillian Haskins, _____, _____, Robert May, _____, _____, Joe Velez, Mike Lanasa, _____, Philomina Ciroti, _____, _____, Joseph Curran, Deanna Cobo, Mary Halik, Michael Barrett, John Bernreuter, Gregory _____, Francis Hernandez, Nancy Conley, _____, _____,

2nd Row L to R: _____, Francis Hernandez, Nancy Conley, _____, _____, Julie Hendrick, Gladys Nicolau, Carol Hardin, John Ranaldo, Bob Bernreuter, Fred Haskins, Robert Jabour, _____, Robert Bonamy, _____, _____, _____, Steven P _____, _____,

3rd Row Standing: Jamie Loomis, Cory McDonald, _____, Ted Zorsky, Frank Orta

BJBernreuter collection

110

In 1958, Father Mike Cronin, SJ, celebrated his sixtieth year as a Jesuit. He was dearly beloved by all, especially those attending daily Mass and who had to be at work early. Serving as his altar boy for many Latin rite Masses throughout the fifties, it is my recollection, and I may be a little off, that he could celebrate a Low Mass in 12 to 15 minutes, whereas a High Mass might have taken as long as 25 minutes. In his eighties, Fr. Cronin was also very hard of hearing, so many chose to confess to him.

In 1958 the church was closed for a short period while the termite eaten floors were replaced by terrazzo. The Chi-Rho cross, copying the pattern from the altar, was inlaid into the terrazzo floor in the narthex of the Church. New pews were added increasing the seating capacity from 400 to 600.

The MIHS Student Council presented the school with a five foot high, white cast-iron statue of the Blessed Virgin Mary and a circular fish pond to be placed in front of the convent.

**1959**   The Rectory, also a victim of the elements, was found to be inadequate for the growing needs of the parish and was replaced by the present modern structure in April of 1959. This restoration was made possible by the hard work of Father Beaver, SJ. The Very Rev. Coleman Francis Carroll, Bishop of Miami, in his first official capacity in Key West,

came to dedicate it. (Because the Jesuits had held back contributions to help fund the new Diocese of Miami, to which they now belonged, it is rumored that the bishop was not pleased with the "elaborate" rectory built by these Jesuits and nicknamed it the 'Jesuit Hilton')

In 1959 Father Lester F. X. Cuterl arrived to assist the pastor. A swimming pool was also added to MIHS this year thanks to generous donations from the community.

That year's attendance for the Catholic elementary schools was as follows:
- Convent of Mary Immaculate – 549
- St. Joseph's School – 410
- St. Francis Xavier School – 150

Saint Theresa's Hall was constructed on the Convent grounds at a cost of $50,000 to increase the number of classrooms and provide a canteen and social hall for the high school.

Both the St. Francis Xavier School and the St. Joseph's School buildings had exceeded their capacity by 1959. A new school was desperately needed, so Father Beaver initiated yearly Bazaars and other fund raising events for the new St. Mary Star of the Sea School, which would be an all-inclusive elementary school for boys and girls. People of all faiths and walks of life assisted Father Beaver in making the drive a tremendous success. With St. Francis Xavier School gone, many black families inquired about where their children were to go to school. Fr. Beaver told them, "Just show up on the first day of school." And with that statement a huge step was taken in Key West.

**In this photo you can see St. Theresa's Hall to the left of the convent where the old government building had been and the auditorium is to the far right. The new rectory is behind the church.**
**Monroe County Public Library**

**1960**    Father Robert E. Nilon, SJ, arrived to assist Fr. Beaver this year, and Mary Immaculate High School hired Charles (Dutch) Shultz as the schools first paid coach. With a lot of heart and in spite of the limited number of boys enrolled, he launched the school's first basketball season.

Hurricane Donna ripped through the middle of the Keys on September 9th. A category 4, this was the fifth strongest storm ever to hit the United States. The storm destroyed just about everything from Marathon to Tavernier. Although untouched by the ravages of the storm, Key West was without water and electricity for many days as the power lines and water pipes were severely damaged. Those without cisterns or well water would bathe at the beaches or during rain showers. The Convent, however, was blessed with good well water and the Church and Rectory were served by a huge cistern behind the Church.

**1961**    The unsuccessful invasion of about 1,500 Cuban exiles on Apr. 17, 1961, occurred in the Bahía de Cochinos (Bay of Pigs) on the south coast of Cuba. The US complicity in the training and arming of these militants to overthrow Castro's communist government caused a hostile relationship to develop amongst many Latin American countries towards the United States. Because of Key West's proximity to Cuba, many of the families of the boarders at the Convent, concerned for their wellbeing, had to decide whether to allow them to stay or bring them home. Many preferred that their daughters return home to them, so there was an exodus of sorts to Venezuela and to Puerto Rico. This resulted in a substantial loss of income for the school.

In 1961 Father John J. Millet and Father Thomas J. McGrath arrived as assistants and the parish seemed to be in a continual state of change. Saint Mary Star of the Sea School on Simonton Street, was finally completed at a cost of $167,000.

Focus immediately shifted to Mary Immaculate High School, also a coeducational institution, which was being evaluated by the Southern Association of Colleges and Schools accreditation committee. The school was found lacking in areas of safety and modern educational standards. The school was given a five year grace period to comply or lose its accreditation.

**St. Mary Star of the Sea School**
St. Mary Star of the Sea collection

Because of termite damage and the extensive costs for the repairs necessary to restore the old convent buildings it was decided that restoration was not feasible. It would be simpler and a lot cheaper to tear it down and build a new school. This put the good Sisters in a difficult situation as enrollment (tuition revenue) had declined significantly due to the loss of the elementary girls' school (CMI) to the new diocesan coed school.

Since the political developments in Cuba had drastically reduced the number of resident students (the girls that lived in the dormitory above the auditorium) and the New York Province of the Sisters of the Holy Names was already so heavily encumbered by debt, it was clear that they would be unable to assume further indebtedness.

**Pictures from St. Mary Star of the Sea collection**

The idea of tearing down the Convent was disheartening to all Key West citizens, as it was by now more than a local landmark; it was a cherished institution that served the entire community. It was a monument to who we were and what we had been through. Senator John M. Spottswood, a Conch, personally wrote the Archbishop seeking a means to save this school, once regarded as the most handsome educational building in the State.

Everyone wanted to restore the buildings, but there were no preservation grants available and the projected costs of restoration were astronomical.

The Bishop let it be known that he was seeking real estate elsewhere on the island to build a new high school. That was the final straw. The Sisters would not be able to compete with a new diocesan High School on the island. The loss of this historic building became the impetus for the state to protect buildings of architectural or historic significance.

**1962**   It is ironic that the state historical marker was received that year and installed on the Convent grounds facing the street.

The Provincial Superior of the Sisters met with Bishop Coleman Carroll to negotiate a suitable financial agreement. Simply put, if the high school were to continue, new buildings must be constructed, and the Sisters could not possibly afford such an endeavor.

St. Mary Star of the Sea collection

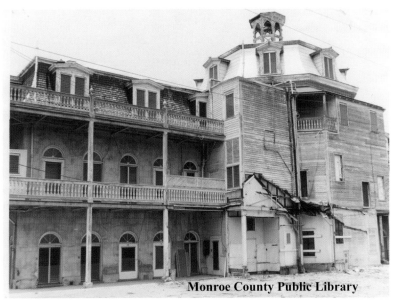

Monroe County Public Library

The Bishop was seemingly unmoved until the realization sank in that the Sisters might have to sell all their property and withdraw permanently from Key West. That would certainly have left a rather large ecclesiastical hole in the parish, both physically and spiritually. Eventually a suitable plan was agreed upon, whereby the Diocese would take out the $600,000 loan and guarantee it for five years. By then it was believed the high school would be able to handle the debt reduction through tuition. This seemed workable until just before the start of construction; at that time the Bishop informed the Provincial that the Diocese would only pay the interest payments for five years, but the Sisters must legally guarantee the loan. The Bishop was adamant, so with no other hope, except a verbal agreement from the Bishop to help if they ran into trouble, the Sisters went forward with construction.

May 5th was a tragic day for our community when the car containing five Sisters, returning from the funeral of Sr. Olive Denise in Tampa, plunged into a canal on the side of the Tamiami Trail. Three were able to exit the submerged vehicle, but Sr. M. Rose Rita (Edna LaVigne) and Sr. M. Georgette (Maria Loiselle) were not. A funeral Mass was held in Key West with Bishop Carroll, priests, brothers, and sisters from throughout the diocese in attendance.

On October 14th, U.S. intelligence photographs revealed missile bases in Cuba and Russian ships en route with obvious ballistic missiles on deck. This began the Cuban Missile Crisis, and Key West was once again forced into the national forefront of potential hostilities. President Kennedy ordered a Naval blockade around the Cuban nation and a major buildup of military forces in Key West. The Casa Marina was converted into the Army barracks; barbed wire was stretched across our beaches with gun emplacements; and Hawk Missile sites were strategically placed throughout the Keys.

Father John Schroeder, SJ, and Father James Loeffler, SJ, arrived in 1962 to assist Father Beaver. This same year central air-conditioning was installed in the Church and was a blessing for the parishioners of this tropical island. It would be a treat for many to get to Mass and cool off.

Even though the US Census for 1970 showed Key West as the only city in the Miami Diocese to lose population from 1960 to 1970, Bishop Coleman Carroll, chose to create the new parish of St. Bede's in Key West. The dividing line between the two parishes was Leon Street. Unfortunately, this also divided the parish by income, with the new St. Bede's Parish inheriting the larger and wealthier areas of Key West. With a school to maintain, a much larger land mass, older structures, and more of them, St. Mary Star of the Sea was soon foundering in debt and relying heavily on the Diocese of Miami to sustain it.

## St. Bede's Parish

Since many of St. Mary's parishioners were now assigned to St. Bede's Parish and eventually were folded back into St. Mary Star of the Sea, I will give a brief rundown of their pastors, administrators, and associate pastors. I know that many loyal parishioners stayed with St. Mary's as this was the church they were brought up in and had received their sacraments in. Also many of either parish would attend Masses at whichever church was most convenient at the time. It is a small town and they were only two and a half miles apart.

St. Bede's Parish was founded on August 16, 1962, with the Reverend William V. Cashman as Administrator. The Rev. Michael Licari took over in February of 1964 and was replaced the following year by the Rev. Anthony J. Chepanis. In August of 1968, Rev. Larkin F. Connolly was assigned as Pastor. Rev. Michael D. Hickey came as Administrator in 1972 and Rev. Miguel Goñi as Pastor in 1974. The Rev. Thomas (Fr. Tony) Mullane arrived as Administrator in 1978 and was assisted by the Rev. Kilian Holland in 1981, the Rev. James Dwyer, Associate Pastor in 1984 and the Rev. George Witt, Assc. Pastor in 1986. The Very Reverend Eugene Quinlan, VF, Dean of the Keys, was transferred from Big Pine Key to Key West, and on June 17, 1987, took over the reins of both parishes.

I can't mention St. Bede's without a Fr. Tony Mullane story or two. Even though parishioners of St. Mary Star of the Sea, my family would often find ourselves at St. Bede's because of the Mass schedule. Father Tony liked to fish and he had a nice boat. Put the two together on a Saturday afternoon enough times and as any 'Captain' knows, something is going to not work right and sometimes that is the engine. I can remember getting updates on Fr. Tony's position as we sat waiting in church for his arrival to begin Mass. Sure enough, about 15 minutes late he would rush in pulling his vestments over his fishing clothes with that elfish grin that said it all, "Great Day!"

Fr. Tony always had a plan... sort of. As soon as he entered the church he would go up and down the aisle randomly selecting the readers for that Mass. No one had forewarning to prepare the reading. His sermons appeared to follow that same pattern. He would start talking randomly about the Gospel reading and it didn't seem to be going anywhere. Then just as I was sure he was totally lost in his thoughts, he would pull it all together in a few short sentences with profound spirituality. I would sit amazed thinking, "How did he do that?"

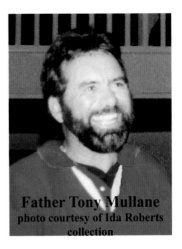

**Father Tony Mullane**
photo courtesy of Ida Roberts collection

### The Second Vatican Council 1962-1965

The Second Vatican Council (also known as Vatican II) set out to define the Catholic Church and its role in today's world. It was the twenty-first Ecumenical Council of the Catholic Church and the second to be held at St. Peter's Basilica in the Vatican. It opened under Pope John XXIII on 11 October 1962 and closed under Pope Paul VI on 8 December 1965.

**1965**    This year the sanctuary was further distinguished by the addition of a separate altar of sacrifice. The original altar, still supporting the tabernacle, remained as the altar of repose. Encouraged by the Church Fathers during the Second Vatican Council, this new altar would allow the priest to celebrate the Mass while facing the congregation.

At a great loss for this parish, Father Beaver left his beloved island home in 1965 as he was transferred to Tampa. He had served his parish and community exceedingly well and would be missed by everyone. He had brought in a new era of community involvement in the support of the church, school, and parish. Known as "Key West's People's Priest", he was accepted by everybody.

*"You could go to a bar mitzvah and there would be Joe Beaver,"* said Kermit Lewin, a former Mayor of Key West. *"I knew him as mayor, as a member of his parish, and as a friend. I knew him since we were kids. In fact, he was instrumental in getting me to run for mayor. He was the greatest guy in the world."*

**Father Joseph Beaver S.J.**
Photo BJBernreuter collection

Father Beaver was also an accomplished pilot. In 1961 he saved my brother's life. Bert, at three years old, ran into the street and was hit by a car. Sustaining major head injuries, he needed to be flown to Miami Jackson immediately. There was no time for an ambulance plane to come from Miami, so borrowing the Toppino family's airplane, Father Beaver was able to fly Bert, with attending medics, to Miami where he was rushed into the OR for emergency surgery. Our family was forever indebted to Father Beaver for his quick reaction and the Toppino family for their generosity in the loan of their aircraft.

Towards the end of his nine years of service to our parish, Father Beaver suffered a stroke and needed someone to drive him around to administer communion to shut-ins. *"He felt bad about that,"* Father Nilon recalled. *"He felt like he was imposing."* Father Beaver died in his sleep at the St. Ignatius Residence in New Orleans, June 25th, 1982, after an extended illness.

**Fr. Robert Nilon, SJ**
Photo courtesy of the Archives of the New Orleans Province, Society of Jesus, Monroe Library, Loyola University, New Orleans.

Father Beaver was replaced by his assistant Father Robert Nilon. Father R. A. Tynan, SJ, came to Key West to assist Father Nilon in 1965 and was followed in 1966 by Father Sal San Marco, SJ, Father John Q. Minvielle, SJ, and Father William T. Dillon, SJ.

Sr. Rose Immaculata arrived as principal of St. Mary Star of the Sea School. A native of Washington, D.C., she came from her last assignment in Silver Springs, Md. This year Wayne (Buddy) Owen, took over the coaching position from Dutch Schultz. He organized the high school's first football team. Only 32 boys reported for the team, mostly eighth graders, which did not allow him to have much depth on his squad. The cost of equipment and team travel, forced the team to disband the following year.

**1966**     Bishop Carroll dedicated the new Mary Immaculate High School in February, and in June, the good Sisters moved into their new modern convent.

**New Convent**

**Mary Immaculate High School**     **Photos by BJBernreuter**

Taking over the reins from Coach Buddy Owen, Mr. William Parker became the first teacher/faculty member to coach the sports teams. Father Joseph LeRoy, SJ, also arrived this year to assist Father Nilon.

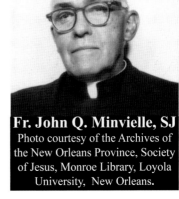

**Fr. John Q. Minvielle, SJ**
Photo courtesy of the Archives of the New Orleans Province, Society of Jesus, Monroe Library, Loyola University, New Orleans.

**1968**    Rev. John Q. Minvielle who had been in the parish since 1966, was promoted to Pastor and served until 1970.

Sr. Helen DuCharme, a native of Cohoes, N.Y., arrived as the new Sister Superior of the Convent. This was the first year that the school would have a separate principal, relieving the superior of those duties. Serving as first principal of the school was Sr. Alice Veronica, a native of New Haven, Conn. A new coach also arrived when Richard Dougherty returned to Key West after 21 years to teach government and English. A college all-star, he brought his skills home to the Mariners baseball and basketball program.

April 21st, St. Cecilia's Music Hall was set on fire, presumedly by some children who were seen playing around the building just before the blaze started. This 70 year old building was originally constructed by the Army as the hospital mess hall during the Spanish American War.

In 1968, due to the tremendous influx of new residents from the northern United States as well as the Caribbean, and also in recognition of Bishop Carroll's dynamic leadership, the 10-year-old Diocese of Miami was made an Archdiocese and named Metropolitan See for all of Florida.

**1969**    The parish community launched a fund raising drive to raise $200,000 to build a multi-purpose gymnasium and cafeteria for the high school. Co-Chairmen for the drive were Dr. Lance Lester and Mr. Norman Artman. Leo Haskins Jr. was the Parish Coordinator Chairman.
The program for this drive lists the MIHS faculty as follows:
Sr. Susan Taggart as Principal, Sr. High Student Council
Sr. Anne Celine as Vice Principal, Sr. HR, Algebra 1,2, Math 4, Latin 2, H.S.
Sr. Helen DuCharme, Jr. HR, Fine Arts, Guidance Counselor Jr. High
Sr. Pamela Brion, 10th HR, Eng 10,11, Latin, Journalism, Forensics
Sr. Mary Catherine Clements, 9th HR, Eng 9,12, Reading, Journalism, Foren.
Sr. Jeanette LaPlante, 8th HR 101, 7&8 Language Arts, Spanish I
Sr. Eileen McCarthy, 8th HR 102, History, Geo, Am History, Jr. H Student C.
Sr. Jean Trainor, 7th HR 104, 7&8 English, Reading, Book Store
Sr. Margaret Mary Schick, 7th HR 103, 7,8,9 Science, Drill Team, Sci Club

Sr. Mary Winifred, Jr. & Sr. Art
Sr. Agnes Anne, French, Chorus & Music
Sr. Christina Mary, Librarian, Library Club
Mr. Steve Alscher, World & Am History, Phys. Ed., 9th Gr Bus, 7th Religion
Mrs. Linda Boyd, Phys. Ed., Cheer leading, Pep Club, GAA
Mr. Richard Dougherty, Phys. Ed., Government, Civics, Coach
Mr. Carl Gabriel, Guidance Counselor Sr. High
Mrs. Grace Gutierrez, School Secretary
Mrs. Maria Lopez, Spanish 1,2,3,4
Mrs. Charles Malby, Phys. Ed.
Mr. Arthur Moran, 8th Grade Math
Mrs. Norma Renner, Home Economics
Mr. Ronald Sallengs, Chemistry, Business, Math, Phys. Ed.
Mr. Allan Sosnow, Biology, Chemistry
Mrs. Joan Wolfinger, Typing, Record Keeping, Business Law, Shorthand 2

**Sr. Louis Gabriel (left) Sr. Sup. Theodor Theresa (center) and Sr. Theresa Cecilia (right) demonstrate the changes to SNJM habits.** Photos St. Mary Star of the Sea collection

1969 marked a decade of change, not only throughout South Florida, but for the entire country. In the early sixties Cuban refugees began pouring into Key West because of the spread of communism in Cuba. The Vietnam War was building up and dividing the country. The Cuban Missile crisis had put all of America on watch, and we were nationally in a race for the moon with our avowed enemy, the Russians. Vatican II changed the perceptions of our religious and laymen alike and to many it seemed to confuse their defined offices. And finally, the Civil Rights Movement gained the momentum needed to change the culture of our schools, politics, and workplace.

Locally, St. Mary's parishioners watched as the new altar was added, the old convent buildings were torn down, and St. Cecilia's Hall burned to the ground. The Diocese of Miami was made an Archdiocese and Bishop Carroll elevated to an Archbishop. Change had come fast and this was just the beginning, as the hardest hits were yet to come to this small island.

# Chapter 10
## A Diocesan Parish

**1970**     After 120 years of devoted service to the people of Key West, the Jesuits turned over the Parish of St. Mary Star of the Sea to the Archdiocese of Miami. As stated by the Jesuit Provincial of New Orleans, the Very Rev. John Edwards, SJ, ***"The Jesuits are supposed to go into a place where they are needed and stay for as long as they are needed. And when the Bishop of a Diocese feels he is capable to take over a particular parish, unless there are peculiar reasons otherwise, he really has an obligation and a perfect right to do so."***

And so Key West's last Jesuit Pastor, Father John Q. Minvielle and his assistant, Father Leo G. O'Conner, turned over the reins of "St. Mary's" to Father Charles Zinn, the previous Chancellor of the Archdiocese, and his assistant, Father Emilio Martin.

More than 300 religious, civic, and military leaders, with the citizens of Key West honored the departing Jesuits and welcomed the new Pastor at a reception sponsored by the Catholic Daughters of America, Court St. Mary Star of the Sea. The Grand Regent of the Catholic Daughters of America, Mrs. Irene Tait gave this testimony:

***"Like the ripples of a pebble tossed into the sea, some things cannot be measured until the last wave comes into shore. So it is with the endeavors of the Jesuit priests who have labored in the Vineyard of the Lord in Key West during the past 72 years.***

***"The people of Key West have been the beneficiaries of their unselfish devotion, their untiring labor, their ardent zeal in the name of Jesus. We may say farewell, but we can never say goodbye, for the Jesuits are a part of the history of Key West and its spiritual development that cannot be erased.***

***"They walk across the pages of every family album, are indelibly written on the front pages of family Bibles and engraved on the records of so many baptisms, marriages, and deaths that only when the last one is read can we begin to tell the glorious history of the Jesuits in Key West."***

L-R: Fr. Charles Zinn (new Pastor), Mrs Mary Watson, Mrs. Irene Tait (G. Regent CDA), V. Rev. John Edwards (Provincial of So. Provence of Jesuits), Mrs. Pat Rung, Fr. John Minvielle (last Jesuit Pastor), Mrs. Mary McCurdy, and Fr. Rene Gracida (Chancellor of the Archdiocese.) Photo courtesy of St. Mary Star of the Sea collection / appeared in the Voice Miami Fl 1970

Annually, from 1964-1969 the Provincial Superior of the SNJM's visited Archbishop Carroll to review the financial status of the school, reiterating that the Province could not assume the loan obligations of MIHS if the school was not producing the tuition resources. It had become increasingly clear that the school could not meet the semi-annual payments (approximately $50,000) that they were obligated to this year.

At a meeting with the Archbishop on December 14th, he stated his proposal:

1.      The Archdiocese will take title to all the property involved, (the new convent, high school, and youth center).

2.      The Archdiocese will assume the entire loan obligation.

3.      The high school must become a diocesan high school.

4.      The Sisters must guarantee a staff of a fixed minimum number.

5.      The Sisters can have their own administration, such as is done by other high schools which are run by religious orders, in the Archdiocese.

The museum artifacts that had been removed from the old Convent were loaned to the East Martello Museum and the Lighthouse Museum.

The new multi-purpose cafeteria and gym was completed and dedicated by Archbishop Carroll who had contributed $50,000 to the development fund for the building. Today this is known as Sacred Heart Hall.

Photo by BJBernreuter

**1971**      At a final meeting of early January, the Sisters stated that they were prepared to yield to the Archdiocese all property rights requested, in view of the Archdiocese assuming the total debt of construction in 1965. They also asked to be compensated for investments in the property and cost of construction for three existing structures that they had paid for.

On March 15, the final agreement was reached; in effect the Sisters had to release to the Archdiocese all buildings and land held by them in Key West, in exchange for the Archdiocese assuming the total loan obligation of approximately $850,000 over the next 15 years, and responsibility for the school as a diocesan high school. The sisters were to remain and staff the school to the best of their ability. Archbishop Coleman F. Carroll of the Archdiocese of Miami presided over the formalities of the change of jurisdiction.

Later in 1971 Father Aloysius Lucking arrived as assistant pastor.

### Festival Bazaar being planned

Tuesday evening the planning meeting for the Conch Town Festival Bazaar was held at the Rectory of St. Mary Star of the Sea church. Pictured, left to right, (seated) Roger Braun, general cooridnator; Mrs. Herman DeMerritt, honorary chairman; Fr. Charles J. Zinn, general chairman; (standing) Mrs. Eugene Paska, purchasing chairman; Mrs. John Bernreuter, organization chairman; and Mrs. Robert Cooper, booth coordinator.

**Key West Citizen Feb 20, 1972**   **BJBernreuter collection**

Over the years St. Mary Star of the Sea Parish was able to build and sustain the schools with fund raisers such as carnivals and, during the sixties and seventies, the annual Bazaar. This was always a huge parish effort which found many of the same team leaders organizing the benefit each year. The planning team pictured above only scratches the surface of those involved. The newspaper article goes on to list Mrs. Gina DeMeritt as that year's Honorary Chairperson; General Cochairmen were Fr. Charles Zinn and Fr. Larkin Connolly. Advisory Chairmen are Fr. Szczesny, Fr. McFadden, and Fr. Kaiseer. General Coordinator was Roger Braun, Organization Chairperson was Mrs. Joan Bernreuter, and Mr. Leo Haskins was Production Chairman. The Booth Chairperson was Mrs. Nancy Cooper and Mrs. Ana Weekly was in charge of Activities. Other committee Chairpersons were Mrs. Gladys Paska - buying, Mrs. Nancy Cooper - decorating, Mr. Anthony Albury - electrical, Mrs. Joan Bernreuter - financial, Fr. Zinn - building, Mr. Leo Haskins - contributions, and Mrs. Joyce Perez - telephone. These committees would meet for months prior to each Bazaar and it would take days to set up and take down. They were held on the NCCS grounds during the sixties and moved to the High School grounds in the seventies.

**1972**     Later in the year Rev. Jan Januszewski would take over the reins of the parish from Fr. Zinn with Father Todd Hevia as his assistant.  The football program was reinstated that year at MIHS, with another first for the state and maybe the nation, as Theresa Dion, wearing jersey #63, made the boys high school varsity team as their place kicker.  Coach Bill Zumberis said, "She's not only the best we got,  She's as good as anybody's got."  The baseball team won the Class C State Championship that year also with Bill Zumberis coaching. (Pictures pg. 179.)

**1973**     Father Vincente Herrara-Ruis was assigned to the parish as an assistant.

Photo courtesy of Nancy Cooper

### Light of Christ prayer group

In January of 1973 the Light of Christ prayer group was formed under the auspices of Father John McFadden, a Navy Chaplain, and a core group comprised of Nancy Cooper, Donna Dean, Patty Cabrera, and Jim Meek.  Initially, meetings were held at the Navy BOQ, then later at St. Mary's school library.

Through Fr. McFadden, they learned of the Catholic Charismatic Movement.  They attended Days of Renewal in Miami and were exposed on a larger scale to the Gifts of the Holy Spirit.  In June a small group of five traveled to Notre Dame where the inner fire of the Holy Spirit was truly awakened within them.

When school closed that summer, Fr. Michael Hickey invited them to move their meetings to St. Bede's Church.  That same month Father John McFadden invited his friend Monsignor Vincent M. Walsh from Philadelphia, to visit and instruct the prayer group.  All eighteen members of the group had a Pentecostal experience as Monsignor prayed over them individually.

**1974**    A year later, Father McFadden was transferred to Norfolk, Virginia and the Lord called up another leader for the group, Jim Meek. During this time, Father Brendan Dalton arrived as an assistant to the pastor. He joined the Light of Christ Community and asked them to pray over him. This they did, releasing the power of the Holy Spirit within him, and from then on he became their Spiritual Director. Jim Meek was serving in the Air Force and eventually he also was transferred, at which time Nancy Cooper assumed the mantle of leadership.

Enough cannot be said about the impact of this ministry on our parish. Since the formation of these prayer warriors the hospitality and spirituality of St. Mary Star of the Sea has blossomed and is noted by visitors and locals alike in the celebration of Mass. The Light of Christ Community has deepened the faith of all who have participated, and been a source of God's grace with their monthly healing Masses.

Rev. Patrick McDonald was assigned pastor in 1974 with assistants Father Brendan Dalton and Father Raphael Pedroso.

**1976**    In 1976 under the direction of a new pastor, Father David L. Punch, the altar was carpeted and the wrought iron railings removed, as were the tester and the drapes on the altar. Father John McLaughlin was assigned to the Catholic schools. That year, once again the high school dropped the football program.

**1977**    Father Anthony J. Mulderry arrived to pastor his first parish. An excellent speaker, he gave us very insightful homilies made even more charming with his Irish brogue. He was dearly loved by the parish and is always warmly welcomed by his many friends when he visits. On December 8, The Feast of the Immaculate Conception, Archbishop McCarthy arrived in Key West to concelebrate the 125th anniversary Mass of St. Mary Star of the Sea Parish.

**Fr. Tony Mulderry and Archbishop McCarthy concelebrating the 125th Anniversary Mass.**
St. Mary Star of the Sea collection

Fr. Mulderry would make the following changes to the interior of the church: the canopy over the altar was removed, the wall behind the altar painted a simulated marble, and the baptismal font at the rear of the church was also removed. He had as his assistant Father Brendan Shannon and Father Richard Velie, who was assigned to the school. After three years absence, Sr. Dolores Wehle returned to Key West as Principal of St. Mary Star of the Sea School.

**1979**     Father Miguel Guevara arrived as assistant. A visiting priest, (Father) Joe Wesley was arrested by the FBI. Claiming to have been a lawyer before entering the priesthood late in life and now suffering from terminal cancer, he was actually Edward T. Cocomise, a fugitive wanted for robbing a bank in North Carolina. Fooling everyone, he served at both St. Bede's and St. Mary's Churches.

Under their new coach, Tony Herce, the MIHS baseball team won their division championship that year, and for the first time in Florida, a girl, Teresa Kraus, played on a boys varsity team. "Yes," coach Herce said, "she's that good or I wouldn't play her." Football fans were also pleased as their efforts finally returned the program to Mary Immaculate High School.

**1980**     Key West's proximity to Cuba put it in the national spotlight once again, as scores of refugees fled the island nation from Mariel harbor seeking freedom from communism. Known as the Mariel boatlift, the five month hiatus in the life of South Florida brought 125,000 refugees to our shores, most arriving in Key West. Our own fishing fleet, shrimpers, offshore captains, and small open craft, were chartered out to Cuban immigrants who surged into the keys trying to secure a vessel to tender their relatives from Cuba to the United States. On May 7, three weeks into the boatlift, Archbishop Edward A. McCarthy arrived to celebrate Mass in a Navy hanger for the 4,000 refugees being held there.

On June 13, 1980, the Old Island Restoration Foundation President, Fred Cole, presented a check for $2,000 to Father Mulderry to aid in the restoration of St. Mary's. The church underwent cleaning, refurbishing, and a protective coating was put on the exterior of the church.

St. Mary Star of the Sea School was closed at its Simonton and Virginia location and reopened in the renovated buildings at the rear of the High School as Mary Immaculate Star of the Sea School. The vacated school property was then put up for sale to relieve the parish debt.

In early September of that year someone forcibly entered St. Mary Star of the Sea Church and smashed the unlocked tabernacles on the two side altars. They unsuccessfuly tried to open the main tabernacle where the consecrated hosts were kept. Some stereo equipment was stolen from the back of the church.

**1982**     Father John O'Leary became pastor in 1982 and during the year removed six rows of pews to extend the sanctuary out into the church. He also had the entire sanctuary carpeted. The side statues of Our Lady de Cobre and the Infant of Prague were removed and placed in the rear of the church. His assistants were Father Richard Monaghan, O. Carm. (Order of Our Lady of Mount Carmel), and Father Michael Brosnan, CSR, (Congregation of the Most Holy Redeemer). Father Dan Fagen was assigned to the School. In 1983, Father Daniel Jensen, MM, (Maryknoll) arrived to assist Father O'Leary along with Deacon John Noonan.

**Fr. John O'Leary**
**Michael's First Communion**
BJBernreuter collection

Although most of his changes were not popular with the parishioners, Father John was a very spiritual man. He introduced the Catholic Cursillo to our parish. The Cursillo Movement, which began in Spain in 1944, came to the United States in 1957 as an "instrument of Christian renewal to form and stimulate persons to engage in evangelizing their everyday environments." The Cursillo, or "little course" is an intense three day program which continues indefinitely on the fourth day, sustained by weekly Ultreyas.

Under Fr. O'Leary's direction, George and Dorothy Sherman organized volunteers from the parish to provide a Soup Kitchen to serve the increased numbers of people asking for food. Utilizing the Renewal Center's kitchen they were able to serve these poor souls with dignity, five days a week.

Blessed Marie-Rose Durocher, foundress of the Sisters of the Holy Names of Jesus and Mary, was beatified in Rome by Pope John Paul II on May 23, 1982, and her remains are now at the Co-Cathedral of Saint-Antoine-de-Padoue, in Longueuil, Quebec. Born Eulalie Durocher in Saint Antoine-sur-Richelieu on October 6, 1811, she died 38 years later, on October 6, 1849, just 19 years before the Convent in Key West was erected. A relic of Mother Marie-Rose is currently displayed and venerated in the Convent adoration Chapel of Divine Mercy.

**1983**     After 115 years, the services of the Sisters of the Holy Names of Jesus and Mary in Key West came to an end with the departure of the last nun, Sister Dolores Wehle. Sr. Dolores, principal of St. Mary's School, had served the community for eighteen years. With regrets to the community of Key West, Sister Virginia Dunn, S.N.J.M. the Provincial Director, announced that due to staffing problems, the Sisters of the Holy Names, would not be able to continue their mission on the island.

Sr. Dunn further states *"...we look over a long and blessed history that extends back to 1868 when our Sisters came to Key West. We experience a deep sense of gratitude to God for calling us to the island and to you... Our sincere interest and long commitment among you, the people of Key West, motivate us to express our openness to future service should we have Sisters available... With affection we know Key West as 'The Rock". With you we pray that the Lord who is 'Our rock' and our salvation' will continue to be with you. May God's presence give you great hope and may God bless the efforts of parish and archdiocesan leaders who work with you in promoting Catholic education in Key West."*

**Sr. Dolores Wehle**
St. Mary Star of the Sea collection

This was a sad blow to the good people of St. Mary's Parish and Key West. The Sisters were always held in the highest esteem and loved dearly by people of all faiths on the island. Archbishop Edward McCarthy made the following response, *"With all members of the Church of Key West, my heart is heavy as the Sisters of the Holy Names terminate their devoted service in the name of Christ to the people of this beloved community.*

*"The Sisters have been very much a part of the life and history of Key West. They have been the revered teachers of its children, of all ethnic groups, but more they have brought the example and the solace and the care and the joy of Christ's love to the community in good times and in bad."*

St. Mary's Thrift Shop and the N.C.C.S. Hall were set afire by an arsonist and burned to the ground in December of 1984. Built by the Knights of Columbus it had been used as a U.S.O. during World Wars I and II, a library, a meeting hall for church functions, and most recently, as a storage facility for the thrift shop. James Johnson turned himself in claiming he did it because he was upset by the 'hippies' and transients who were using the building to sleep in. The building and church property was in the process of being sold to the Wengroup Corporation for development as a pedestrian mall, townhouses, and shopping center.

Father Valerian Alonso, SJ, visited us and served the parish for a short time in 1984. In 1985 Father John J. Boyle spent time with the parish and in 1986 we were blessed by the visit of Father Frank Gallogly, OSA, (Order of St. Augustine), who came several times to visit our community. His spirituality and love endeared him to many in our parish.

**1986** Archbishop Edward A. McCarthy ordained Key West resident Kirby McClain, as a Permanent Deacon of the Catholic Church, in a special ceremony at St. Mary Star of the Sea Parish Church, May 4, 1986. He became the first deacon in our parish's history. A retired Navy Captain, Deacon Kirby and his wife Angela first moved to Key West in 1950 and retired here in 1980 after receiving the Meritorious Service Medal, the Navy's second highest peacetime award. Captain McClain was an accomplished Navy pilot and worked on the Mercury Space Program.

His sermons were well thought out, delivered with authority, yet tempered with humility, and in conclusion

**Deacon Kirby McClain**
St. Mary Star of the Sea collection

Deacon Kirby would pause, look up from his notes and most tenderly say, ***"God loves you... He really does."*** For me, those words summed up every gospel reading, every homily, in fact the whole Mass, and will be forever written in my heart.

The Archdiocese decided to close the High School in 1986, after years of debate, many tears, and financial struggles to keep it going. As president of the P.T.A., I met with Archbishop McCarthy, along with others interested in saving Catholic education in Key West, and against the wishes of his chancellor, he granted us funding for as long as he could and withheld the closing of the elementary school.

Low enrollment was the main cause for closing the High School as it had dwindled to the point where the Archdiocese no longer felt it prudent to subsidize the efforts. Even though anticipated, the actuality was still a shock to the parish. The burden of going through the procedures and bearing the displeasure of the parish fell on Father John O'Leary and the Very Rev. Eugene M. Quinlan, pastor of St. Peter's parish in Big Pine Key. Father Quinlan, as Dean of the Keys, accepted the responsibility sadly and assisted Fr. O'Leary in the transition. June of 1986 saw the last graduating class of Mary Immaculate High School. Mary Immaculate Star of the Sea School was then moved into the high school facilities.

## Scandals Rock the Church

By the mid-eighties allegations of clergy abuse and cover-up were becoming widespread nationally and worldwide. It was a time when so many good and devoted priests were disparaged because of the actions of a small percentage. This was not just a Catholic issue, although the media made it seem that way. These same evils would be found in the public school system, in sports programs at major universities, the Boy Scouts of America, and in all other religious faiths. For all our many good priests here is a quote from 1 Peter 4:12-17.

**"Beloved, do not be surprised that a trial by fire is occurring among you, as if something strange were happening to you. But rejoice to the extent that you share in the sufferings of Christ, so that when His glory is revealed you may also rejoice exultantly. If you are insulted for the name of Christ, blessed are you, for the Spirit of glory and of God rests upon you. But let no one among you be made to suffer as a murderer, a thief, an evildoer, or as an intriguer. But whoever is made to suffer as a Christian should not be ashamed but glorify God because of the name. For it is time for the judgment to begin with the household of God; if it begins with us, how will it end for those who fail to obey the gospel of God?"**

When I gaze at the corpus upon the crucifix the image is not clean and beautiful. No... Jesus's body looks filthy, beaten, and bloodied. This is the Sacrificial Body of Christ. The body He gave up for us.

Our Church, founded by Jesus the Christ, is His body living today. We are that Church, also sinners, bloodied, and broken; we are the Church Militant. We are in the battle, for our own souls and the souls of others, and, make no mistake, it is a spiritual war.

Is the Church perfect? Consider this: didn't one of the 12 apostles, handpicked by Jesus, betray Him and the others? Did Jesus make a mistake? Peter was rebuked by Jesus many times, and then three times he denied Jesus and yet was still chosen as our first Pontiff.

**"And so I say to you, you are Peter, and upon this rock I will build my church, and the gates of the netherworld shall not prevail against it. I will give you the keys to the kingdom of heaven. Whatever you bind on earth shall be bound in heaven; and whatever you loose on earth shall be loosed in heaven."** Matthew 16:18-19

Yes, the Catholic Church has made mistakes, some popes have made bad decisions, and a very small percentage of priests have sinned grievously. Do you think this surprises God? We are all frail humans, all sinners, all in need of God's great mercy. We are the scourged body of Christ, but... we are called by God to forgiveness, to stay the course in our faith, and as Christians we remain under the protection of the Holy Spirit.  And best of all… we know the ending, because we read the Book.

And how has our Catholic Church responded?  The United States Conference of Catholic Bishops (USCCB) mandated changes and instituted programs such as the Charter for the Protection of Children and Young People which pledged the Catholic Church in the U.S. to provide a "safe environment" for all children in Church-sponsored activities. The thrust of the charter was the adoption of a "zero tolerance" policy for sexual abuse.  The Charter instituted reforms to prevent future abuse by requiring background checks for Church employees. The Charter also requires dioceses faced with an allegation to alert the authorities, conduct an investigation, and remove the accused from duty.

By 2008, the U.S. church had "trained 5.8 million children to recognize and report abuse with diocesan programs like, Protecting God's Children and Virtus, etc. It had run criminal checks on 1.53 million volunteers and employees, 162,700 educators, 51,000 clerics and 4,955 candidates for ordination. It had trained 1.8 million clergy, employees and volunteers in creating a safe environment for children."

These initiatives were very much needed and changed the way we do things in our own parish.  For instance we were very liberal in allowing anybody, clergy, lay ministries, etc. to use our Renewal Center resources for meetings, retreats and such.  Now we have to be more careful.  We require certificates of proper training and compliance; everyone needs to be screened.  Every person in our parish and school system that has any contact with children or access to any area that might interact with children has to undergo this tight scrutiny including fingerprinting, background checks, and continuous training by the archdiocese.

**Sue Barroso, the Parish Facilitator for Virtus, trains our teachers, parents, students, and any who might come into contact with our children for any Parish activity.**   Photo by BJBernreuter

# Chapter 11
## Spiritual Renewal

**1987**     The previous twenty years of national turmoil, followed by the upheaval within the Diocese, the combined losses of the Jesuits and Sisters of the Holy Names of Jesus and Mary, along with the dramatic changes within the church itself surely inflicted a deep wound in the psyche of the parishioners. Almost every vestige and symbol of their faith had been overturned or removed. Namely, the dramatic renovations to the church which removed the wrought iron testers, the baptismal font, communion railings, and precious statues from the side altars. These changes were hard to endure for many of the older parishioners, who had worked so hard to build the church and sustain it over the years.

During this same period, the parish was divided to form St. Bede's, which left deep scars on members of both parishes, and finally the closing of Mary Immaculate High School. Now rumors were rampant that St. Bede's was to be closed and become a mission parish. Both parishes were in turmoil and in need of strong leadership and a healing heart. How would the people of such a close-knit island community, after struggling so many years to build and support their traditional ideals within the parish, find the strength and will to move on, savor what they could, and keep their faith alive?

They did it the old way, the way they had always overcome the obstacles of the past: through love and hard work. This parish had not survived 135 years of poverty, war, and isolation without developing a resiliency of character which allowed them to survive. And they did more than survive. Taking stock in their holdings, searching for what they could do, and realizing that in the end, it was not the edifice of the church that mattered, nor where the statues were placed; it was not the altar railings, baptismal font, or whether the priest faced them or not during the celebration of the Mass; it was and always had been, their faith in God, and their personal outpouring of love that mattered.

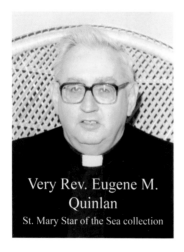

Very Rev. Eugene M. Quinlan
St. Mary Star of the Sea collection

On June 17, 1987, the Very Rev. Eugene M. Quinlan became Pastor of both St. Mary Star of the Sea and St. Bede's parishes. As the new Pastor, he began the difficult process of pulling together a divided community which, along with their pain, were now mistrustful of the clergy.

On April 16, 1988, St. Bede's parish was officially merged with the parish of St. Mary Star of the Sea under Father Quinlan and a great healing had begun. Father Quinlan combined traditional authority with a soft touch and was able to accomplish a great deal in a very short time. He brought the two

parishes together and he listened with his heart. He had the stature to sway the Archdiocese in many matters and the empathy to appease the wounds of many parishioners. A lesson had been learned and, like Israel wandering in a spiritual desert, God was keeping His closest watch. And now that the trial was over, the statues were returned to their original places of honor and Fr. Quinlan began a restoration of the church property and his parishioners' confidence in the clergy. His assistant was Father Edward J. Rizzo in 1987 and in 1988 he had the lovable Abbot Gregory Roettger, OSB, (Order of St. Benedict) and Father Mark Mages, OSB.

Fr. Quinlan had a unique ministry to AIDS patients. He would spend many nights at the hospital with dying young men. Even though he was not in good health himself, it never interfered with his pastoral duties. He was instrumental in securing the building of St. Bede's for AIDS Help and served on their board for many years.

Under his guidance he had the graves of the priests who were buried in the Catholic Cemetery restored and a new fence added. Fr. Quinlan also began a Memorial Day Mass at the cemetery and each September he would invite Bishop Roman down from the Archdiocese to celebrate the feast of Our Lady of Regla with our Cuban community. The "Virgin of the Rule" is highly venerated in the Cuban City of Regla and also Havana.

**1989**     Aware of the parishioners' love and respect for the Sisters of the Holy Names of Jesus and Mary, Father Quinlan moved their burial ground from the back quarter of the property, behind the abandoned swimming pool, to a more suitable place of honor. So for the second and last time the eighteen nuns were reverently moved to a beautifully prepared area, next to the grotto which they had constructed in the early twenties.

Photo by B.J.Bernreuter

Their tombstones were all refinished and span one hundred years: the first Sister interred in 1869 and the last to be buried was in 1969. On a humorous note, it was found that one of the nuns had a quarter in the pocket of her habit. Father surmised that even though she had taken a vow of poverty, her family training had prevailed, and she must have always kept a quarter to make a phone call home. Even though she's home now, Father let her keep the quarter.

Responding to an invitation from Father Quinlan the previous year, the Sisters of the Holy Names of Jesus and Mary prepared to return to Key West and re-establish their ministry on the Island.

Four Sisters were chosen and each reflected on the mission as follows:

*"I consider it a privilege in my personal history to go where the spirit of my sisters has been alive for so many years and to have the opportunity to minister and be ministered to by the members of Saint Mary Star of the Sea Parish and the people of the island."* Sister Eileen Kelleher.

*"I'm exhilarated. It's a joy and privilege to be part of this , to join in a journey shared over the years by so many SNJMs, wonderful lay leaders and others. It is a gift of God to be invited and welcomed so warmly."* Sister Audrey Rowe, who had previously taught for 8 years in Key West.

*"On past visits to the Island, I always dreamed of living and working in Key West."* Sister Mary Pat Vandercar.

*"The call to Key West resonates deep within me. I am grateful that the people have kept alive the spirit of our foundress, Blessed Marie Rose Durocher. I am both honored and thrilled to be among those returning to ministry on the island. I believe this reestablishment or refounding of our more than a century of Key West ministry is of God and for God's glory. I believe God is calling forth a new creation in this ministry and is challenging us to be daring and courageous, full of hope, joy and peace."* Sister Dolores Wehle, who had previously spent 18 years serving the Parish in Key West.

Sisters of SNJM return    St. Mary Star of the Sea collection

The Sisters of The Holy Names of Jesus and Mary visit Key West to discuss their return. Standing in the back row are: Sr. Dolores Wehle, Fr. Eugene Quinlin, and Sr. Mary Pat Vandercar. In front are: Sr. Eileen Kelleher, Sr. Rose Gallagher, Sr. Kathleen Ann Humphries, Provincial Sr. Kathleen Griffin, and Sr. Audrey Rowe.

Father Quinlan asked Sister Mary Pat Vandercar and me to document the history of our parish. I researched the history through newspaper articles, documents, and books; while Sister contacted the archivists of all the dioceses that our parish had belonged to throughout its history. She also obtained journals of the Sisters of the Holy Names which gave us direct insight into their sojourns here. Unfortunately, the Sisters were here less than a year when unforeseen issues evolved which resulted in their departure once again.

Continuing his restoration, Father Quinlan closed the chapel for a year to replace the roof and repaint the inside. He was also successful in having St. Mary's church declared and listed as a National and State Historical Site. This was followed by securing state funds for the restoration of the church and so began a long project to unite the parish in the restoration of St. Mary's.

**1991**    Fr. Quinlan's failing health did not allow him to see the project through and he was reassigned to the parish of San Pablo in Marathon. After Hurricane Andrew devastated South Miami in late August of 1992, Fr. Quinlan was assigned to Christ the King Church, to help rebuild their parish. Later he was reassigned to Marathon followed by a move to Queen of Heaven Parish in North Ft. Lauderdale. His last move was a medical retirement to Indian Harbor Beach.

On September 18, 1991, Rev. Gerald F. McGrath was assigned as the temporary Administrator of St. Mary Star of the Sea, followed in a few weeks by the duties of Pastor.

**1992**    Father McGrath's installation by Archbishop Edward A. McCarthy occurred on March 20, 1992. Continuing the path charted by Father Quinlan, he began his tenure with a thorough cleaning of the parish. The wall along Truman Avenue

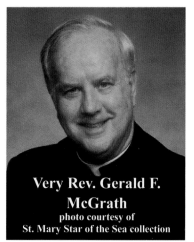

**Very Rev. Gerald F. McGrath**
photo courtesy of
St. Mary Star of the Sea collection

was pressure cleaned, the rectory repainted, the grounds and buildings were inspected, and a plan generated for renewal. The highest priority was given to the continued restoration of the main church building. As the Church and campus were enhanced one could sense the renewed spirit of the parish.

During the summer, Fr. McGrath enlisted the help of three young men, Sean Rousseau, Bill Ayers, and Dean Yates from St. Charles Borromeo Seminary in Philadelphia, Pa. They visited homes, talked with people, and overall opened up a Pandora's box of invalid marriages, unbaptized children, and non-practicing Catholics. Because of their efforts we began to see an increase in parishioner enrollment and many people returning to church and the reception of the sacraments.

Father McGrath initiated a program of "Stewardship as a Way of Life", to the faithful of the parish. Initially there was some resistance to the first phase of the program, but people were asked to make a "Leap in Faith" and consider returning to God a portion of what was rightfully His. The response that first year was overwhelming, with nearly 40% of the registered parishioners "Tithing" at some level, working toward the biblical norm of 10%. This enabled the Pastor to recommend to the Pastoral Council a plan to fund the renovation of the church.

When finally approved by the council and the people of the parish, the major restoration began in earnest. Through it all Father McGrath took great pains to insure the preservation of its inherent beauty and historical nature. On the Feast of the Birth of Mary, September 8, 1992, Mass was celebrated in the newly renovated Church. Archbishop McCarthy came to officially bless the church on December 17, 1992.

**Sisters of the Daughters of Divine Charity
Sr. Georgene Golock, Principal
and Sr. Carmella Chojnacki**
St. Mary Star of the Sea collection

That same summer, Fr. McGrath had contacted two Sisters of the Daughters of Divine Charity, who agreed to come to Key West, Sr. Georgene Golock, FDC, as principal, and Sr. Carmella Chojnacki, FDC, as a second grade teacher. This necessitated making some changes in the convent building, which up to this time had been in disuse, portions of it being rented out to local organizations. One wing was completely redone to make apartments for the two Sisters. This was completed at the same time as the church renovation. The remainder of the convent was then converted to make private rooms for retreats and missions, since the building would now be called the Spiritual Renewal Center.

To protect the newly painted interior, especially the hard to reach ceiling, Fr. McGrath had electric prayer candles installed. These little lights replaced the small candles that were traditionally lit in front of the statue of the Sacred Heart of Jesus which resides in the niche above and behind the left altar. The theory behind this modernization was that there would be no smoke drifting up to the ceiling, which after centuries of use tends to darken the ceiling with soot. Unfortunately, shortly after the church had reopened, an electrical short occurred in the contraption which caused the plastic base and light holders to catch on fire and soon the whole thing was engulfed in flames.

Although no serious structural damage occurred to the building or furnishings, the horrific black smoke, soot, and stench from the melted plastic permeated the

complete interior of the newly refinished church. Every item of furniture, all the pews, the statues, and even the Stations of the Cross had to be taken out, completely stripped, and refinished. The entire interior had to be cleaned and repainted. This was a hard lesson after the parish had waited so long to get back into the church; now we were back to celebrating Mass in the school auditorium again. After the church was fully restored the second time, the candles were brought back into use having proved much safer during their previous hundred and fifty years of service.

According to his office manager Rose Thomas, when Fr. McGrath learned that Key West High School had dropped the baccalaureate service from the graduation ceremonies he re-introduced the Baccalaureate Mass and sent out personal invitations to each graduating senior, a tradition still observed today.

**1993**     Fr. McGrath had contacted Fr. Bill Linhares, a Franciscan priest in Washington, about staffing the center.

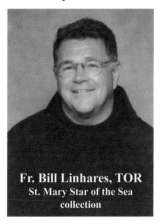

An agreement was reached with the order and Fr. Linhares began his mission as Director of the Spiritual Renewal Center in the fall of 1993. Joining Fr. Linhares to form a small community of Franciscans in Key West were two Franciscan Brothers. Brother John Kerr, TOR, was hired to serve as Director of

Religious Education in the parish. He worked hard in making a solid program for students attending public schools and also served as Youth Director of the parish.

Two seminarians who had worked in the parish for two summers were ordained for the Diocese of Arlington, Va. Fathers Sean Rousseau and Dan Gee. Father McGrath attended their ordinations in Arlington and preached the homily at the first Mass for Fr. Rousseau. Both of these young priests had a tremendous impact on the parish and were instrumental in getting many of our families back to the practice of their faith.

Each year in October and November the "Stewardship as a Way of Life" campaign is renewed. Besides "Stewardship of Treasure", which has continued to benefit the parish and the school, more than 30 ministries have been established with more than 500 members of the parish giving of their "Time" and "Talent" in service to the church and the community.

The prison ministry was newly formed this year; the volunteers would visit the inmates at the Stock Island Detention Center once a week to celebrate the Liturgy of the Word. And the Soup Kitchen started by George and Dorothy Sherman had now grown to the point that the crowd of needy people gathering in the grotto area and next to the school grounds became a concern to Fr. McGrath. The problem was solved by moving the whole operation over to the St. Bede's property on Flagler Avenue. This provided a dedicated kitchen and a large covered seating area.

**1994**    Fr. James Fallon arrived in the winter of 1994 for health reasons. A very spiritual man, Fr. Fallon would usually offer a spontaneous prayer at the beginning of Mass, or after Communion, and always paused for reflection after the homily. He was a charming red headed Irishman, a good listener, and a wise man; but not a morning person. What we will always remember is his sermon each year when he would put the shawl over his head and sing both parts of Tevye and Golde's song, "Do You Love Me" from the musical, *Fiddler on the Roof*. He had a beautiful voice.

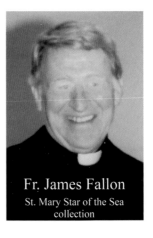

Fr. James Fallon
St. Mary Star of the Sea collection

He served in the Spiritual Renewal Center from 1999 until his death in 2007.

**1995**    In May, the Knights of Columbus Memorial to the Unborn was dedicated by the Rev. Francis X. Dougherty S.J., Council 3652 of Key West. Part of a national program to establish memorials in every diocese, this was the first one erected in the Archdiocese of Miami. Completing two years of hard work, the memorial was constructed next to the Grotto of Lourdes and bears a plaque which reads: **"Keep alive the gift that God gave you when I laid my hands on you."**

2 Timothy 6

Photo by B.J.Bernreuter

Grand Knight Jim Maun concluded the dedication with these words, *"We have all been moved to remember our lost babies. In dedicating this Memorial, we are providing a place for all of the pro-life community to gather and show our grief peacefully and in the spirit of forgiveness as we pray for an end to our national tragedy, abortion.*

Photo by BJBernreuter

## Chapel of Divine Mercy

In the summer of 1995, the convent chapel was completely renovated and re-named the Chapel of Divine Mercy. Five women of our parish were inspired to establish perpetual adoration in this chapel: Sandra Barroso, Sue Barroso, Ida Roberts, Rose Sanchez, and Clara Moore. Among other obstacles they were told that the parish is too small to support such an endeavor. But a month later, on September 8th, Our Lady's birthday, the parish did established perpetual adoration. More than 400 parishioners were involved in giving "One Hour" of their time to be in the presence of our Divine Lord once a week.

Since the beginning of perpetual adoration our parish has risen to a new level of spirituality. The ministries have increased and services extended. In that chapel, in Jesus's presence, spiritual miracles are occurring, hearts are healed, and God's mercy and graces are overflowing out into our streets.

**"This brings it all together,"** Fr. McGrath stated, **"and all else is as nothing. The Lord is with us."**

Service to others is one of the attributes of good stewardship. Parishioners now serve in Ministries to the Sick and Shut ins, Prison Ministries, Family and Home Life Ministries, the Eucharistic Ministry, as Lectors, Senior Acolytes, Volunteers to the Homeless, Aids Ministry, Christian Education of Children, the RCIA Team (Rite of Christian Initiation for Adults) and support team for Education of Adults, Bible Study and Adult Education Classes. But the crowning glory of all of our efforts was getting more than enough of our people to volunteer to spend the "One Hour" of their time a week in Perpetual Adoration.

**1996**    Fr. Roberto Garza arrived in June right after ordination. He gave very personal homilies that touched us all. Fr. Garza was loving and caring, and he made you feel good just being around him. He left us after two years and now is the rector, of St. John Vianney College Seminary.

Fr. McGrath &
Archbishop McCarthy
St. Mary Star of the Sea collection

Archbishop Edward A. McCarthy returns to concelebrate St. Mary Star of the Sea's Sesquicentennial Anniversary (150th). This was calculated on an old history of Key West, which mentioned the first recorded Mass occurring in City Hall in 1846. (This event was covered earlier in this book on page 27) This certainly was not the first Mass on the island, as there were missionaries here in the 1700s.

For this event, Fr. McGrath had a group of us complete and have printed the history of St. Mary Star of the Sea. Now, as I rewrite this history, I realize that we didn't reach our 150th year until 2002, and then we missed it. This is peculiar, because our parish was formed in 1852 and celebrated the 100th Jubilee correctly in 1952 and the 125th correctly in 1977. For future reference, our 200th Jubilee will be in 2052 if anyone is paying attention then.

**2000**    On November 18, Peter H. Batty of Key West was ordained a deacon by Archbishop John C. Favalora in Saint Mary Cathedral, Miami. Deacon Peter Batty, baptized in the Church of England in Salisbury, had entered the full Communion of the Catholic Church through the Rite of Christian Initiation of Adults in 1993 which he now directs.

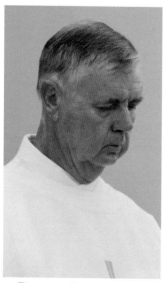

**Deacon Peter Batty**
**Photo courtesy**
*The Florida Catholic*

Deacon Batty has been a blessing to our parish; his sermons are very enlightening and personable. What do I mean by that? I mean he brings God's words to life, giving them meaning in our everyday lives; and most of all, he walks the talk. He is in charge of the prison ministry and Baptismal Classes in English.

During his Diaconate training, Peter and Fr. McGrath discussed better ways to reach out to the poor in our community. This led to Peter's graduate thesis for his master's degree to focus on: "What an outreach to the poor in the city of Key West should look like." He and Fr. McGrath planned to implement such a program before McGrath was reassigned. Father Paco embraced the idea and together, he and Peter actualized the mission. Peter secured the lease for the property on Stock Island with a purchase option. Finally opened in 2006, this project ended up being totally financed by the Klaus-Murphy Foundation.

**2002**    Key West welcomed its new pastor Father Francisco Hernandez (aka Father Paco), who was formally installed as Pastor May 2, 2003. Fr. Paco was assisted for one year by Fr. David Dueppen and then by Fr. Henryk Pawelec. Fr. Henryk was transferred to St. Rose of Lima parish in Miami the summer of 2007, and has since returned as Pastor of San Pedro's parish in Islamorada.

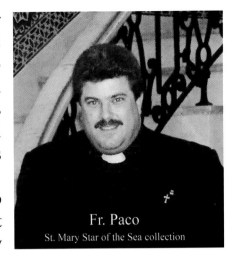

Fr. Paco
St. Mary Star of the Sea collection

Father Paco made many improvements to the parish campus, such as the fountain in front of the chapel, new walkways, the living rosary lawn, and the Stations of the Cross Garden, which is behind the Renewal Center.

**2004**    In the summer of 2004, a rock garden behind the Convent and Renewal Center was transformed into a Stations of the Cross Garden which was blessed by Bishop Felipe Estevez, Auxiliary Bishop of Miami, on December 12, 2004. The Stations are constructed of Carrara marble with mosaics of the scene for each station, all framed in bronze, illuminated with night lights, and placed within a tropical garden.

At the entrance of the Garden is a marble corpus on a wooden crucifix with a marble image of Our Lady Sorrows looking on from the left. This Garden has become a place of prayer for groups during the season of Lent and for individuals night and day throughout the year. Adjacent to a refectory used by the Parish for social events, this Garden along with the seating in the refectory is used for the three extra Masses on Easter Sunday. An estimated six hundred participants may worship in this beautiful space.

Photos by BJBernreuter

Photo by BJBernreuter

Photo by BJBernreuter

**2005**     May 9, 2005 the parish suffered the loss of our beloved Deacon Kirby. With family and friends in attendance on the Navy ship, he was given all the rituals of a Naval burial at sea, befitting his rank and service to his country.

Rev. Richard Rodriquez, a native Conch, was briefly assigned to the parish. Father John Burke was a very holy man suffering the last stages of Alzheimer's disease; he arrived in 2004 and left us in 2005. He was so compassionate towards the poor, he would give away all his money during his daily walks about town.

Hurricane Wilma had been downgraded to a category 3 Hurricane as it passed just north of the keys on October 24th. However the unique path of the storm, its size, and intensity caused severe flooding throughout two thirds of the island, twice. First, as the storm approached Florida, it pushed water across the keys from south to north. Then as the storm finally crossed into the Everglades, all the water that had been pushed north across the bay was released. The tide then raced back across the Lower Keys this second time with a 5 to 10 foot surge and out to sea. As severe as this storm was, the winds over our island were minimal, no lives were lost or buildings destroyed, even though the flood damage was terrible in the low lying parts of the island. Wilma was the most intense tropical storm ever recorded in the Atlantic basin, and the fourth Category 5 hurricane of the record-breaking 2005 season with winds of 185 mph (295 km/h). As a result, Wilma is ranked the fourth most costly storm in United States history.

**Flooding caused by Hurricane Wilma, looking down Harris Avenue, Key West, Florida**
State Archives of Florida,Florida Memory,http://floridamemory.com/items/show/99969 Dale McDonald

**2006**      Saint Mary Star of the Sea Outreach Mission was blessed by the Most Reverend Felipe Estevez, Auxiliary Bishop of the Archdiocese of Miami. Also shown cutting the ribbon is Fr. Paco, City Mayor Morgan McPherson, City Manager Julio Avael, and County Mayor Sonny McCoy

Photo courtesy of St. Mary Star of the Sea

Fr. Seamus Ward arrived in very poor health, and was embraced by the parish. In December, Father Paco was transferred to Immaculate Conception parish.

To help raise funds for the Catholic school, Earl Duncan (Past Grand Knight and Charter member of the Knights of Columbus council) and his family donated a brand new car to be raffled off at the Parish picnic. This began a yearly tradition which they have continued since 2006.

**2007**      Our new pastor, Fr. John Baker, arrived in January, fully immersing himself into the parish. From the outset one could tell he was an organized man. Directing Sue Barroso to list every parish ministry, their leaders or contact persons, and their membership, Fr. John then made a point of attending each of their meetings to further integrate himself into the workings of the parish. He joined the Knights of Columbus Council 3652 and serves as their chaplain. Father also endeared himself to the Religious Education program by making frequent visits to the classrooms where the children relish his humorous interruptions.

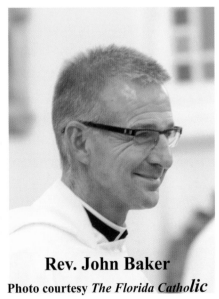

**Rev. John Baker**
**Photo courtesy *The Florida Catholic***

"Management By Wandering Around" or sometimes biking around. Father can be seen day or night walking or biking through our community, visiting the sick at their bedsides, attending meetings, or administering the sacraments. Fr. John is not one to be sitting on his hands. He is all about getting things done.. One of his major projects was upgrading the facilities at St. Mary's School. The building was in poor shape and the classrooms needed a face-lift. The school staff worked wonders and brought the school into compliance with the Florida Catholic Conference Accreditation Program and the State of Florida.

**Sisters of Opus Spiritus Sancti: Sr. Lucy Mworia, Sr. Mary Mushi, Sr. Euphemia Kimario, Sr. Consesa, and Sr. Marietha Kimaro,** photo courtesy of Julie Hendricks

**2008**        Sister Lucia Mworia, Sister Mary Mushi, and Sister Marietha Kimaro, all Opus Spiritus Sancti Sisters arrived from Tanzania, Africa, to serve our parish. Sr. Lucia was a Medical Doctor and was the leader of this small community of Sisters who graciously entered into just about every ministry of the parish. They joined the Catholic Daughters of the Americas, taught at St. Mary's School and the Religious Education program, filled in many hours of adoration, worked in the Outreach Mission, the Food Kitchen, as Extraordinary Ministers of the Eucharist, the choir, and so much more. They have expressed over and over again their love for the people of our parish and their joy in serving here.

The Parish School "Board of Management" was drafted by the efforts of Father Odhrán Furlong, on sabbatical from Ireland, in the spring of 2008. The board is based on the Irish School System and consists of the pastor, the parish manager, the principal of the school, two teachers, two parents, and two members of the community. Their duties are to consider any ideas, complaints, projects, or school involvement from parents, teachers, or the parish.

The School Management Board, the Finance Committee, and the Pastoral Committee, advisory boards mandated by Canon Law and formed in the years 2009-2010, brought ownership of the church and school to the parishioners.

As always one of the biggest hurdles the parish has to overcome each year is the financing of the Catholic school budget and it always comes down to enrollment, tuition, and, is it worth the expense to keep the school going? It has always been recognized that Catholic schools are the mainstay to nurturing our faith and sustaining growth in the church. But at what costs? That has always been the dilemma. But now the three parish boards have jointly made the commitment and the "money decisions" necessary to finance the school. It is through this "will" of the parish that the school now forever belongs and will be maintained by the parish.

And this is how it worked: the teachers took a voluntary pay cut of 10%, the Sisters of the Holy Spirit took a 50% stipend cut (This theoretically was not allowed, but they stood firm in their decision as it was based on their commitment to serve our parish, not to obtain funds for themselves or their families. They insisted that if others could take pay cuts they would also), Father Seamus Ward took a 100% cut in his stipend from the parish. These heroic efforts, plus the fund raising by our community, saved the school.

The final act of parish ownership was the renaming of the school to St. Mary Star of the Sea School. Although taking the name 'Mary Immaculate' out of the school name broke with tradition, all agreed that giving it the parish name would set for all time the fact that this is not a separate entity, as it had been in the past, but rather it was in fact a part of the parish and would be forever maintained and supported by the parish. Now a Basilica School, it is raised to another level.

Photo by BJBeernreuter

**Outreach Mission**
On the left is:
Laura Bercean, Raquel Rojas, and Roger Morse
*Photo courtesy of The Florida Catholic*
At right is Tom Callahan, Executive Director of the mission.
*Photo courtesy of The Florida Catholic*

The Outreach Mission on Stock Island far exceeded its mission statement to, **"provide goods and services to the indigent and underprivileged residents of Key West Florida. We will do so with respect and compassion, and at no cost to these individuals, without regard to race, creed, or religion".** Fr. Baker acknowledged that, while the church knew there was a need in the community, it wasn't until we responded that we discovered exactly what that need was. This has brought the mission to a whole new level of response that has gone far beyond what St. Mary Star of the Sea originally offered. It is now, thanks to Tom Callahan, a fully 501(c) 3 charitable organization that involves the whole faith community of Key West and utilizes public grants and agencies. More than 20,000 needy people are supplemented with food subsidies each year allowing them to live and work in this expensive environment.

With humble beginnings handing out sandwiches from the trunk of a car many years ago, the Soup Kitchen now operates seven days a week, 364 days a year. Under the direction of Angela McClain, the soup kitchen serves one hot meal a day plus a bag lunch "to go" providing 2000 calories a day, seven days a week, to approximately one hundred patrons each day.

**Chris Morgan, Steve Vach, and Pat Coward**
Photo by BJBeernreuter

**Angela McClain**
Courtesy of A.McClain.

They welcome all who come to eat and treat each with the dignity that is theirs as God's children. This Soup Kitchen is supported by the parishioners, by most of the churches and temples in Key West, by restaurants, by government grants and by the good will of thousands.

Rev. Craig Malzacher, who did his Pastoral Year here in 2006, was ordained a priest in May 2009. Rev. Andrzej Pietrazko was shortly followed by Rev. Lesly Jean as assistants to the pastor.

**2010**      On June 1st, Archbishop Thomas Wenski was installed as the fourth Archbishop of Miami and the first native of South Florida to serve as the Ordinary. A week later he celebrated a Mass of Welcome at Saint Mary Star of the Sea Church, June 8, 2010. Little did our parish suspect how great an honor this man would pursue for our community just two months later.

**2011**      Our Seminarian, Javier Barreto, began his 5th year of Seminary and is now at St. Vincent de Paul.

The Rev. Seamus Ward S.J. passed away in Key West on Tuesday, Feb. 22, 2011. Father Seamus, a Jesuit, served in various parishes, universities and schools in Ireland from 1969 until 1988. He then went to Ethiopia to work with the Jesuit Refugee Service. He continued this work in Ireland, Cairo, Rome, Ethiopia, Sierra Leone, Somaliland, and Mali before returning to Dublin to serve further in their pastoral care until 2005. He came to Key West in 2006 to restore his health.

**Fr. Seamus Ward, SJ**
Photo by Tom Oosterhoudt

Fr. Seamus was well studied and could discuss theology brilliantly. According to Fr. Baker, Fr. Seamus embodied the ideal of his role model Blessed John H. Newman and lived his message concerning the need to appeal to the population at hand… in this regard, aware of the significant Spanish population here in Key West, he went home for one summer as usual and learned to speak Spanish. He was 72 at the time. He was active in supporting the Soup Kitchen. He had a genuine love for the people, and they returned this life giving love back to him.

Fr. John Baker recalls that he was a good colleague and a good priest, *"He was feisty and generous, and Key West brought him to life. He loved the people and they loved him, and each year he would stay longer. When I learned of the "Basilica" petition I called Fr. Seamus in Ireland and asked if he would come to Key West early to help. Graciously he accepted and this allowed me to concentrate on finishing the petition in the required time.*

*That winter Seamus fell and was hospitalized. We realized his time here was drawing to an end. A half hour before he left us, I asked him to send me a sign if our petition was going to be accepted. He did and it was."*

Fr. Francis X. Doughtery Council 3652

The Knights of Columbus completed the renovation on the convent laundry room in 2011. This was the last remaining remnant of the original convent buildings. Designed by Knight Bob Turner and renovated by contractor and Knight Roger Morse. This new Knight's Hall was named in honor of one of the most faithful and hardest working knights: Sir Knight Charles "Chuck" Malby.

Sir Knight
Chuck Malby

**Father Alfredo A. Rolón**
Parochial Vicar

All photos this page by BJBernreuter

St. Mary Star of the Sea was blessed by the assignment of Father Alfredo A. Rolón. He came to us from the Parish of the Little Flower in Coral Gables. He arrived in time to lead the procession of the 400th Anniversary of the Virgin de la Caridad de Cobre in September of the following year. An important Cuban Catholic tradition, the march from the San Carlos Institute to the church was organized by Felix Pradas-Bergnes.

# Chapter 12
## A Minor Basilica

St. Mary Star of the Sea, her beacon shines brighter than ever, guiding her weary wanderers through the dangerous shoals of life to a safe harbor.

**2012**     160 years, have passed since our parish was formed in 1852. St. Mary Star of the Sea has been blessed with a rich and colorful history which now culminates in the distinguished honor of being designated a Minor Basilica. In this chapter you will learn how this distinction began, what it means to the parish, and what comprised the petition to the Vatican to achieve the status of Minor Basilica.

### The Basilica. How did it start?

It started with an e-mail to Father Baker, the night of August 4th, 2010, from Archbishop Wenski, which asked if St. Mary Star of the Sea would consider applying for the honor of being designated a Minor Basilica. Father John remarked that he just sat there staring at the screen – stunned, blown out of the water just thinking about the concept. Then asking himself, "What is a Minor Basilica and just what does that entail?" His reply was, "Yes, yes, and yes!" and the return message came back, "It is not that easy. I'll be in touch."

The Basilica was all Archbishop Wenski's idea from the start. He was born in West Palm Beach, raised in Lake Worth, and attended St. John Vianney Minor Seminary in Miami. So he was well acquainted with this area of South Florida. He knew the history and he knows our parish. His own discipline allowed him to understand the breadth and depth of our parish faith. Thus the idea really came from the parish itself; the people here have ownership in the spirituality, the history, and even the buildings and beauty of the parish. So in a sense the parish community fostered and nourished the idea of a Minor Basilica by what it accomplished and what it has become. In other words it was already, in reality, a Minor Basilica even if not by designation. Archbishop Wenski recognized that and understood his role as bishop was to identify and promote the actualization of the official designation.

The biggest challenge was to form a Basilica Petition committee and hold them to secrecy for the duration of the selection process. The committee members were assigned different sections of the petition to complete, according to their area of expertise. As Archbishop Wenski already knew, this could be a long process and his experience in past petitions taught him that the process could have a negative impact on the parish if people's expectations were not met in a timely manner or possibly not met at all. He did not want that to happen here.

After the committee was chosen, Archbishop Wenski initiated the formal petition to the Vatican to have St. Mary Star of the Sea declared a minor basilica and recognize its historical importance to Catholicism in South Florida.

**What is a Minor Basilica?**

"Basilica" is a title of honor bestowed on a church of historical and spiritual importance by the Holy Father. Churches honored with the title basilica belong to two classes: major and minor. There are only four major basilicas and they are all in Rome: St. Peter's, assigned to the Patriarch of Constantinople; St. John Lateran, the cathedral of the pope, the Patriarch of the West; St. Mary Major, the Patriarch of Antioch; and St. Paul Outside the Walls, the Patriarch of Alexandria. St. Mary Star of the Sea is only the fifth basilica in the entire state of Florida, the 73rd minor basilica in the United States, and unites with more than 1,500 other minor basilicas throughout the world.

The designation confers upon the church certain privileges giving it precedence before other churches (not, however, before the cathedral of any locality). Also included is the right of the conopaeum (a baldachin resembling an umbrella; also called umbraculum, ombrellino, papilio, sinicchio, etc.) and the bell (tintinnabulum), which are carried side by side in procession at the head of the clergy on state occasions, and the wearing of a cappa magna by the canons or secular members of the collegiate chapter when assisting at the Divine Office. In the case of major basilicas these umbraculae are made of cloth of gold and red velvet, while those of minor basilicas are of yellow and red silk, These colors are traditionally associated with both the Papal See and the city of Rome.

The status of being a basilica also confers the right to include the papal symbol of the crossed keys on a basilica's banners, furnishings, and seal; and the right of the rector of the basilica to wear a distinctive mozzetta over his surplice. Other privileges concern the liturgy of the celebration of the concession of the title of basilica, and the granting of a plenary indulgence on certain days to those who pray in the basilica.

**The Minor Basilica Petition:**

To be named a minor basilica, a church has to demonstrate that it deserves the rank by establishing the church's historical significance, architectural uniqueness, and spiritual characteristics. This document imposes on basilicas the obligation to celebrate the liturgy with special care, and requires that a church for which a grant of the title is requested should have been liturgically dedicated to God and be outstanding as a center of active and pastoral liturgy, setting an example for others. It should be sufficiently large and with an ample sanctuary.

It should be renowned for history, relics or sacred images, and should be served by a sufficient number of priests and other ministers and by an adequate choir.

Father Baker described the process, which required answering 120 questions in Latin, as **"A hybrid of a doctoral thesis, a grant application, and a coffee table pictorial book. We had to separate fact from fiction and document everything."** It was accomplished very quietly, with the help of a select group of parishioners and archdiocesan officials. It is a miracle in itself that a secret of this magnitude could have been held by so many for so long.

**The Petition Committee:**
• Secretary Kathy Kolhage: Numbers of baptisms, weddings, parishioners, archivist research, times of Masses, and daily Mass schedule.
• Parish Manager Zack Bentley: All measurements of objects and place.
• Deacon Peter Batty: Liturgy of the Hours and Liturgical year's events, education formation including school, CCD, RCIA, Lenten Missions, and Social Outreach.
• Music Director Kathy Roberts: Music with the three choirs and cantors.
• Bob Bernreuter: History of the parish.
• Tom Oosterhoudt: Photos based upon the texts and booklet.
• Tom Pope: The definitive description on the architecture.
• Felix Pradas-Bergnes: The design of the insignia with the ancillary help of many.
• Father John Baker, pastor: Devotions, statues, religious objects, etc.
• So many others, not listed, contributed their expertise in various ways.

**The characteristics cited in the petition:**
• St. Mary Star of the Sea's status as a national and state-designated historic site. Its roots date back to the 16th century, when Florida was a Spanish territory and the island of Cayo Hueso fell under the auspices of the Diocese of Havana, Cuba. Most of those early settlers were "migratory fishermen from Cuba," and the history of the church, along with that of Key West, has been intertwined with that of Cuba since those early days.
• Today, the parish has sizable populations of Hispanics, not just from Cuba but from Nicaragua and other countries in Central and Latin America. In addition, a considerable population from Poland has recently joined the parish.
• St. Mary Star of the Sea also is the site of one the first Catholic schools in the state of Florida, founded in 1868 by the Sisters of the Holy Names of Jesus and Mary, who served at both parish and school until 1983. In 1986, the high school closed, but the elementary school continues to this day.

- St. Mary Star of the Sea is also a place of pilgrimage for Catholics from other archdiocesan parishes; for college students from campuses elsewhere in the U.S. who engage in mission work during spring and winter breaks; for archdiocesan seminarians and priests seeking a quiet place of reflection; and for the black Catholic youth choir, which travels there each year.
- "Slaves were baptized by the Jesuits" at the church despite civil segregation laws, the petition noted. Also, "may we not overlook the local pilgrimage from the local people of Key West … (who) desire to find peace in this place with 283 bars."
- St. Mary Star of the Sea serves 1,300 registered families — Key West has about 30,000 year-round residents — as well as approximately two million visitors who come to Key West each year, about a quarter of whom are estimated to be Catholics.
- "We welcome these 500,000 Catholics to our church each year," said Father Baker. "Our Mass assemblies are often divided in half between residents and visitors."
- The parish also ministers to Catholics in the military bases and annexes that are located on the island. The nearest Catholic Church is 30 miles away, St. Peter's in Big Pine Key.
- In addition to Father Baker, the parish staff consists of a Jesuit priest from the Province of Dublin, a permanent deacon, a Marist brother of the New Orleans Province who works at the school, and three Sisters of Opus Spiritus Sancti from Moshi, Tanzania who serve both the parish and school.
- A perpetual adoration chapel, the Chapel of Divine Mercy, has been open since Sept. 8, 1995, and more than 500 parishioners are involved in devoting an hour each week to prayer before the Blessed Sacrament.
- For 35 years, the parish also has operated a soup kitchen for the homeless that now feeds 100 people a day, seven days a week.
- Since 2006, St. Mary Star of the Sea Outreach Mission on Stock Island has served the working poor of the community by allowing them to obtain food, clothing, furniture, prescription drugs and referrals to other social service agencies. The mission served 22,000 people last year.

**The History cited in the petition:**
A substantial part of this history was the basis for the historical background of the church used in the petition.

**The Architectural Significance of the church submitted in the petition:**
Thanks to the professional expertise and research of Tom Pope a

Leone Battista Alberti's
San Francesco Church, Rimini, Italy
Wikimedia Commons (BJB Scan)

St. Mary Star of the Sea circa 1947, State
Archives of Florida, Florida Memory, http://
floridamemory.com/items/show/67774

comprehensive portrayal of the building, along with comparisons to some of the most architecturally admired churches in Italy, were able to be presented in the petition. In 1905, St. Mary Star of the Sea became the first non-wooden place of Catholic worship in South Florida. The church's exterior design represents the eclectic period of American Victorian Architecture and is reminiscent of a modified early renaissance revival building with rusticated exterior walls, round arches, and lunettes filled with transitional Gothic arches, louvered shutters and colored glass windows.

The stone blocks that went into its construction are in fact poured concrete made from the oolitic limestone dug from the ground on which the Church stands. It became the first non-wooden place of Catholic worship in South Florida. The exterior architecture is similar to Leone Battista Alberti's San Francesco Church in Rimini, Italy.

Capped with a cross, each tower rises 29.57 meters (97 ft.) high. The towers' bases are 3.96 meters (13'8") square with louvered shutters at the ground level. French windows with arches filled with decorative colored glass are at the mezzanine level and fixed louvers with a lunette decorated with Gothic tracery are at the attic level of the towers. The towers are crowned with very steep pitched conical roofs covered with metal tile shingles.

The left tower serves to encase the bell and the carillon which call God's people to prayer at the Hours and for the Masses. The bell, 1.22 meters (4 ft.) in diameter and 1.1 meters (3 ft. 6 in.) in height, was manufactured by the American Bell and Foundry Company in Northville, Michigan, No. 48.

A later gift to the church, it was installed in 1918 and is inscribed with these words:

**To the greater honor and glory of God, this bell is donated
by Mr. & Mrs. J. A. Kelly, of Chicago
to the Church of the Blessed Virgin Mary
Immaculate Key West, Florida,
Michael Joseph Curley
being Bishop of the Diocese of St. Augustine
Florida in the year 1918.**

Although taken out of service in the 1960's the bell still resides in the steeple. Its clapper has been removed and now hangs on the back wall of the church next to the sacristy door. Access to the bell is from the choir loft, through a trap door in the ceiling.

I remember once pulling on the rope to ring the bell in the fifties. It was not easy for a light lad as it is big and heavy. I can't imagine the effort it took to raise it up there so many years after the church was built.

Particular care was taken to have the church comfortable and cool in this sub-tropical climate, as this was a time before air-conditioning was available.

Photo by BJBernreuter

Photo by BJBernreuter

For this purpose, six of the nine exterior bays are defined by paired shutters and doors which measure 1.22 meters (4 ft.) wide by 2.99 meters (9 ft. 8 in.) high, with arched colored glass windows rising to a full height of 5.03 meters (16.5 ft.) These high and wide doorways were set along the east and west walls instead of windows, to provide refreshing cross ventilation in the nave. In Key West we have the ability to leave these doors open throughout the year due to the pleasant climate.

Providentially, these open doors also provide more space for the faithful to gather during the busy winter and spring tourist seasons. Although the church can seat 500 comfortably, with its wide central nave measuring 14.97 meters by 19.42 meters (49 ft. 10.5 in. by 63 ft. 7 in.), the two side aisles allow another 200 to stand within the Church, and with the doors open, another 200 can assemble on the surrounding sidewalks for a total gathering of 900 souls.

Passing under the entrance portico, which is not the original, we encounter the striking front doors made of Dade County Pine (a native hardwood which is termite resistant and now virtually extinct). Along with the portico, the narthex serves as a gathering area as people arrive for liturgical celebrations. The narthex has two marble holy water fonts and is adorned with an inlaid mosaic of terrazzo with the symbols of the Chi-Rho cross flanked by the alpha and omega.

Above the narthex and extending into the nave is the choir loft. It is large enough to accommodate our three choirs together for major liturgical celebrations, along with our organ and piano, but originally it held a grand pipe organ, parts of which still adorn the rear of the loft.

The interior of the church inspires one with its clarity and height and is also representative of the American Victorian Architecture. Many elements of the interior have both Romanesque and early Renaissance characteristics reminiscent of Filippo Brunelleschi's Santo Spirito Church in Florence, Italy.

**Filippo Brunelleschi's Santo Spirito Church in Florence, Italy. Wikimedia Commons (BJB Scan)**

**St. Mary Star of the Sea interior
Photo by BJBernreuter**

The nave ceiling is a simple flat barrel vault decorated with rare pressed metal panels. The ceiling rises 9.54 meters (31 ft. 3 in.) above the terrazzo floor, which was originally a wooden floor (replaced because of severe termite damage). The ceiling is supported on an arcade of round headed arches and tall thin cast iron columns with foliate Romanesque capitals. Selective decorative elements are gilded, which emphasizes the height of the columns and ceilings.

The altar of repose consists of seven types of marble and previously served as the altar of sacrifice. Below the tabernacle on the altar of repose is a marble and gold leaf mosaic of the Chi-Rho cross flanked by the alpha and omega. The four marble columns and their capitals on the front ends of this altar repeat the Romanesque style of the columns and capitals originally constructed in the nave of the Church.

Photo by BJBernreuter

This altar is attached to the floor and is considered a fixed altar, therefore it was dedicated and according to church traditions it had the relic of a martyr or saint placed under the altar. There is a small repository, about two by four inches and approximately an inch and a half deep in the center of the altar table and directly in front of the tabernacle. It is not known what or whose relic was placed in this altar as that information may have been lost or destroyed over the years. Unfortunately, the repository has been cut open and the relic that was there has been removed; by whom and when it was removed is unknown. Perhaps, it happened when the altar was changed to an altar of repose and the new altar of sacrifice, facing the congregation, was dedicated. The present one, being constructed of wood and not being a fixed altar, does not contain a relic.

[**Author's Note:** The altar in the Divine Mercy Chapel does contain a relic. However it is not known who the relic is from, but I am still researching.]

A tabernacle, also of Carrara marble, with an inlaid decorative mosaic in the cap is securely fixed on the altar. The front brass tabernacle door depicts in relief the Annunciation of the Archangel Gabriel to the Blessed Virgin Mary with the presence of the Holy Spirit and the inscription: ET VERBVM CARO FACTVMEST. (THE WORD WAS MADE FLESH ) — John 1:14 (See detail in front of book.)

A masterly carved crucifix, whose origin is unknown, rises above the tabernacle. The natural light, playing through the colored glass arches on both sides of the nave, adds special significance to the stained glass window over the altar. Although there are devotional statues and images throughout the Church,

Photo courtesy of *The Florida Catholic*

photo by B.J.Bernreuter

and nature blazes with glory through the open doors, the clarity of the lighting and integrity of the furnishing compels the pilgrim's eye to move forward to the altar of sacrifice, then, up to the stained glass image of Stella Maris, and finally up to the heavens in transcendence.

There are 30,191 year round residents within the Parish's region. An estimated 8,500 of the residents are Roman Catholic. There are 1300 families who are committed to stewardship of time, talent and treasure for the well being of the Church and the Parish.

Five thousand of these residents are military personnel and their families of the five military installations, annexes and bases within the Parish boundaries for which there are no Catholic chaplains.

Key West is a tourist destination. In 2010 there were 2, 230, 999 visitors to this Island. According to the City statistics, 1,165,327 visitors stayed overnight, 206, 263 were day trippers and 859, 409 were cruise ship passengers who docked in the ports and disembarked to visit. It may be presumed that 24 percent of these visitors are Catholics in conformity with the national percentage of Catholics. Our Church attendance is often divided in half between residents and visitors.

**Sacred Heart of Jesus**

**Our Church is gifted
with many statues and
icons reflecting the piety
and devotions of our
diverse community**

**Virgen de Guadalupe**

**St. Joseph
(From 1st. Church.)**

**Our Lady of Mount Carmel**

**Black Madonna of
Częstochowa, Poland**

All photos by BJBernreuter

**St. Anthony of Padua**

159

**Infant of Prague**

**La Virgin de la Caridad de Cobre**

**The Apostle St. Jude Thaddaeus**

**St. Francis of Assisi**

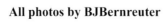

All photos by BJBernreuter

# *Petition Granted*

**Archbishop Thomas Wenski**
*Photo courtesy of The Florida Catholic*

"**Last year, I made the request for this honor through the Holy See's Congregation for the Divine Worship and Discipline of the Sacraments and, at that time, I submitted the necessary documentation as to why St. Mary Star of the Sea, was worthy of consideration,**" Archbishop Wenski said in a video shown at all the Masses the weekend of February 11, 2012. "**This beautiful and historic church becomes the first minor basilica in the archdiocese and only the fifth in the state of Florida.**"

"**This designation is ultimately the consequence of your faith in Jesus Christ, and the faith of those who have been here before us,**" said Father John Baker, in his homily to parishioners that weekend.

Father Baker's new title is Rector of the Minor Basilica of St. Mary Star of the Sea. He recalls that soon after becoming pastor in 2007, he noticed a certain "good energy" or "karma" of holiness around the historic parish. "But what is the name for it?" he wondered. He believes Archbishop Wenski captured it precisely, two months into his tenure as archbishop of Miami, as he began securing for the church the status of minor basilica. "The ecclesial word, which describes precisely, what you and I and he sense and perceive, at St. Mary Star of the Sea, is faith en-fleshed in love, which gives hope to others."

The archbishop noted that its status as a minor basilica now makes St. Mary Star of the Sea **"The Pope's 'Parish Church' here in the archdiocese,"** and as such, **"Should link all Catholics here in South Florida most closely to the person of the Holy Father.**

**Father John & Deacon Batty**
*Photo courtesy of The Florida Catholic*

"**In naming a church a basilica, it is kind of making it like the Pope's church, so that if the Pope ever showed up in Key West, he could feel at home here at St. Mary Star of the Sea,**" said Archbishop Wenski.

"**The history of Key West is also the history of the parish of St. Mary,**" said Deacon Peter Batty of the new basilica. "**But I think one of the reasons that the Pope chose to bestow us with this singular and wonderful honor is because of our presence in the community today.**"

(All copy this page is from Archdiocese of Miami Web Site. www.miamiarch.org/)

## The Basilica Mass

**Photos all courtesy of *The Florida Catholic***

The procession began in the foyer of the school and proceeded through the Stations of the Cross Garden, along the walkway next to the Rosary Lawn, and then into the Basilica.

It was led by the KoC Color Corps, followed by the Sisters carrying the tintinnabulum, representatives from each Parish Ministry, former and visiting priests, the KoC Council members with the ombrellino, the Knights and Lady of the Holy Sepulchre, the concelebrants, Father John Baker, and Archbishop Thomas Wenski.

The procession entering the church was led by the KoC Color Corps. Commander Bob Bernreuter leads, Faithful Navigator Ed Bunting on left, Sir Knight Jim Maun PFN on the right.
Photo courtesy *The Florida Catholic*

The tintinnabulum is carried by Sr. Mary Mushi, OSS with Sr. Dolores Whele & Sr. Theresa Cecelia SNJM. Erica Hughes is following, and accompanying them are Fr. Ken Whitaker and Lazaro Enriquez from the Archdiocese.
Photo courtesy *The Florida Catholic*

KoC members Chris Weber, Andy Kirby-with ombrellino, and Robert Delauro
Photo courtesy of *The Florida Catholic*

Many former priests who have served the parish were here, Fr. Francisco (Paco) Hernandez, Fr. Anthony Mulderry, Fr. Ohdran Furlong, Fr. Jerry Morris, and Fr. Mario Castanado.
Photo courtesy *The Florida Catholic*

The angels in heaven could not have sung as beautifully as our three choirs did that evening.

The Mass began and the liturgy was spiritual and very traditional. It was the epitome of how a Catholic Mass is celebrated. There was incense, prayers, the liturgy of the word and the liturgy of the Eucharist. Christ was present in all of His Glory.

And His people were gathered as one flock. And all of the ministries were represented filling up one fourth of the Basilica.

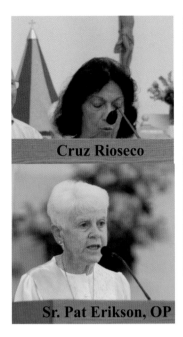

Cruz Rioseco

**Doug Lynde - Deacon Batty - Wally Moore**
All photos on previous page and this page are courtesy of
The Florida Catholic

Wladysla Bujak

Rosaling Dhaiti

Sr. Pat Erikson, OP

**Bringing up the gifts: Cross bearer is Steve Saunders followed by Capt Patrick Lefere, US Navy, Capt Aylwyn Young, USCG, Comdr Gary Tomasulo, USCG, and John Parks, Usher.**

**Knights and Lady of the Holy Sepulchre
Sir Bernard W. Wolff, Lady Delores Wolff,
and Brother Bud Luks.**

# Homily preached by Archbishop Thomas Wenski
## May 31, 2012 at the dedication of the Minor Basilica of St. Mary Star of the Sea in Key West.

Photo courtesy of *The Florida Catholic*

We gather today, on this feast of the Visitation of Mary, to give thanks for the favor shown to this historic parish church dedicated to Mary, Star of the Sea, to the Key West community and to our archdiocese. We are all extremely grateful that Pope Benedict XVI has seen fit to raise this church to the status and dignity of a minor basilica.

As a basilica, besides the ombrellino and the tintinnabulum, the special umbrella and bells, Mary, Star of the Sea, is granted the privilege to display the coat of arms of Vatican City on its façade and the crossed keys of St. Peter on all its furnishings and liturgical appointments. Having in the Archdiocese of Miami a basilica does underscore the special bond that joins this local Church to the successor of St. Peter. The unity that should exist among those who invoke the name of Jesus – that unity for which Jesus himself prayed – is realized cum Petro and sub Petro: with Peter and under Peter.

In today's feast of the Visitation of Mary, which was just described for us in the Gospel reading, we see exemplified the sublime greatness of Mary. Before worrying about herself, Mary instead thought about elderly Elizabeth, who she knew was well on in her pregnancy and, moved by the mystery of love that she had just welcomed within herself, she set out "in haste" to go to offer Elizabeth her help. Mary proclaimed with her whole life what she had replied to the angel at Nazareth: "I am the handmaid of the Lord." Mary's life has been a gift of self to God and to neighbor. And now Mary in heaven carries out a ministry of intercession on our behalf – ever in communion with her Son. And, in Key West, generations of Catholics instructed in the faith by the good priests and holy nuns who served here, heroically braved isolation, storms and disease by entrusting themselves to Mary and her maternal protection.

The Sisters of the Holy Names of Jesus and Mary, especially Sister Louis Gabriel who built the grotto, taught their charges to pray with them the words of the Memorare: "Remember, O most gracious Virgin Mary, that never was it known that anyone who fled to thy protection, implored thy help, or sought thy intercession was left unaided."

A small plaque with a painted image of Mary recovered from the 1901 fire that destroyed the earlier church built by Father Kirby in 1851 had an inscription written by Father Hunincq that describes perfectly the significance of this parish and the faith that has sustained it over the years: **"Since it first shed its light in Key West, it has been like a star of the sea for the wandering mariner; it has been a star of hope and comfort in times of despair and sorrow and a star of joy to those who have lived in its teachings."**

**"Blessed are you among women,"** Elizabeth tells Mary. Yet, Mary remains the humble maiden of Nazareth: She is not weighed down by pride or selfishness. She never forgets that she is the handmaid of the Lord, nor does she forget the gratuitous goodness of God. That we, too, might not forget, the Church entrusts to us her canticle of praise, the Magnificat, which we pray every evening at vespers.

Only by accepting God's love and making of our existence a selfless and generous service to our neighbor can we joyfully lift a song of praise to the Lord. This parish's present commitment to its school as well as this parish's commitment to social ministry, seen in its outreach to the homeless and the hungry, represent "a selfless and generous service to our neighbor" that has always characterized the Catholics of Key West since the very first settlement of this island.

"My soul proclaims the greatness of the Lord." Mary recognizes God's greatness. This is the first indispensable sentiment of faith. It is the sentiment that gives security to human creatures and frees from fear, even in the midst of the tempest of history.

This song of Mary, her Magnificat, is, in the words of Pope Benedict XVI, "an authentic and profound 'theological' reading of history: a reading that we must continually learn from the one whose faith is without shadow and without wrinkle."

Going beyond the surface, Mary "sees" the work of God in history with the eyes of faith. This is why she is blessed, because she believed. By faith, in fact, she accepted the Word of the Lord and conceived the Incarnate Word. Her faith has shown her that the thrones of the powerful of this world are temporary, while God's throne is the only rock that does not change or fall.

With the eyes of faith, we too can see the work of God in the history of this state and this city. We see it in the short-lived mission of the Jesuits in Upper Matacumbe Key in 1568; we see it in the early 1700's when Cuban fishermen living here in Cayo Hueso were attended to by priests traveling from Havana 90 miles away. We can see it in the 1820's in the Catholic faith of Stephen Russell Mallory and his mother – and he, a graduate of Springhill College, would later write his son at Georgetown, urging him to **"cling to your religion, my son, as the sheer anchor of life here and to come. Never permit yourself to question its great truths, or mysteries. Faith must save you or nothing can; and faith implies mystery."** With the eyes of faith, we can see God at work when Mass was celebrated in City Hall in 1846, and when Father Kirby built the first Mary Star of the Sea in the 1850's.

Mary's example of readiness and generosity in the service of others, seen in her visitation of Elizabeth, has been imitated by the selfless and generous service of the priests who died of Yellow Fever while ministering here in Key West. Her example has been imitated during the century long presence of the Sisters of the Holy Names of Jesus and Mary in teaching the young and in ministering to the sick and wounded during the Spanish American War.

As the Second Vatican Council taught, Mary is the Mother of the Church and is therefore the model for us as we try to live our Christian vocation in the world. This Basilica of St. Mary Star of the Sea, the southernmost parish of the United States, stands as a beacon of faith, hope and love. It stands as an invitation written in brick and mortar to all who visit this community – an invitation to trust in God and to imitate Mary in what she herself said: **"Behold, I am the handmaid of the Lord. May it be done to me according to your word."**

Yes, as Pope Benedict says, **"Her Magnificat, at the distance of centuries and millennia, remains the truest and most profound interpretation of history."** For all human history – without faith – is incomprehensible. As the Pope writes in Spe Salvi, **"Human life is a journey. Towards what destination? How do we find the way? Life is like a voyage on the sea of history, often dark and stormy, a voyage in which we watch for the stars that indicate the route… Holy Mary, Mother of God, our Mother, teach us to believe, to hope, to love with you. Show us the way to his Kingdom! Star of the Sea, shine upon us and guide us on our way!"** (Pope Benedict XVI, Spe Salvi)

At the conclusion of the archbishop's beautiful homily the Very Reverend Chanel Jeanty approached the pulpit and recited the proclamation of the Holy Father, Pope Benedict XVI, confirming the designation of Minor Basilica on St. Mary Star of the Sea.

The Very Rev. Chanel Jeanty is reading the proclamation as Tony Herce holds it for all to see.
Photo courtesy of *The Florida Catholic*

Photo courtesy of *The Florida Catholic*

After receiving the proclamation, Father Baker and Deacon Batty present a signed print of a new painting of St. Mary Star of the Sea Basilica to Archbishop Wenski.

Father John holds up the proclamation to the roaring applause of the Parish.

Photo courtesy of *the Florida Catholic*

At the end of Mass everyone gathered in front of the church celebrating with joy all the ceremony they had just witnessed, but this photo, courtesy of *The Florida Catholic*, captures something which illustrates what is so special about St. Mary Star of the Sea. Do you see it? Yes, we can look through the open doors and even see the great stained glass masterpiece over the altar, but that's not it. No, you must raise your eyes up, past the great seal of the Vatican, and there, unnoticed by her children, Our Lady watches over us with love. Every day as we drive by to work or to play, she is watching.

What Robert O'Steen wrote in the Florida Catholic, on the almost 150th anniversary in 1996, pretty well sums up our history as I have sought to portray it in this book.

**"Located on a crossroads of history, St. Mary Star of the Sea Parish has seldom existed as a tranquil paradise, but rather as a participant in the shifting tides of history that swirled all around. The wars, the population influxes, the mortal epidemics and ravages of hurricanes, isolation from the rest of the church until recent times, and shifting ethnic mixes all have buffeted St. Mary's throughout her history.**

**But this Star of the Sea still brightly marks the presence of Catholicism at her southernmost location in the continental United States and continues as a beacon to all who seek a safe harbor in the arms of Christ."**

# *Appendix*

The coat of arms for the new Basilica incorporates key elements reflecting the nature of our Parish.  The position of the sand indicates that this Parish was the beginning of the Archdiocese of Miami and is at the end of it. The conch shell is the traditional symbol of Key West. The Star above the conch shell is for our Patroness, and above the ombrellino the cross stands on a conch pearl.

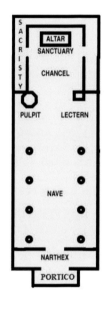

**Basilica Coat of Arms**

**Archdiocese of Miami Coat of Arms**

Photos by BJBernreuter

Coat of Arms of the Vatican

These three symbols are now proudly displayed on the Basilica. Other symbols to be displayed are the ombrilino and the tintinnabulum.  The umbraculum (Latin) or ombrellino (in Italian) means 'little umbrella' and was once used on a daily basis to provide shade for the pope.  Now it is a symbol of the Roman Catholic Church and the authority of a pope over it.  Whenever a pope visits a basilica, its umbraculum is opened.  The embroidery on the lambrequins include the Coat of Arms of Pope Benedict XVI, Archbishop Wenski, the Archdiocese of

**Ombrellino**  **Photos by BJBernreuter**  **Tintinnabulum**

Miami, and the Basilica of St. Mary Star of the Sea; it also displays the seals of the Knights of Columbus, who paid for the ombrellino, and a likeness of their founder the Venerable Father Michael J. McGivney. The Knights of Columbus carried it in and placed it next to the altar during the designation ceremony.

The gold bell on the pole, the tintinnabulum, also signifies the Basilica's link to the Pope. In the Middle Ages it served the practical function of alerting the people of Rome to the approach of the Pope during papal processions. The shape of the bell enclosure is based on the gold medal that Mary Immaculate High School awarded to valedictorians; this is to pay tribute to the work of the Sisters of the Holy Names of Jesus and Mary and the role of Catholic education in creating and sustaining the faith of the community. A Sister of the Holy Names of Jesus and Mary accompanied the Sister of Opus Spiritus Sancti who carried the bell, ringing it all the way through the procession, to place it next to the altar.

# Ministries of St. Mary Star of the Sea in Action

### St. Mary's Youth Group
A Catholic youth organization that performs community service projects.

photo by Greg Barroso

**Ed Sminky delivers the goods for the Outreach Mission**
photos courtesy of Robin & Kevin Beede

**Dana performs to a full house**
St. Mary Star of the Sea collection

**Annual Rock 'N' Roast benefit for St. Mary's School**
John Correa and hatchet crew cutting the pork. Kevin & Robin Beede event organizers.
photos courtesy of Robin & Kevin Beede

# *Ministries of St. Mary Star of the Sea in Action*

## Catholic Daughters of the Americas
### Court No. 634

The largest and oldest national organization of Catholic women in the world. Their members are active in nearly every ministry in the Parish.

Photo by B. Bunting

## Knights of Columbus Color Corps

Fr. Joseph F. Beaver SJ, Assembly 2016 of the Florida Keys. The color corps is the drill squad of the Fourth Degree which adds pomp and ceremony to Parish Masses and activities.

photo by Tom Oosterhoudt

## Catholic Religious Education
### Parish Catechists:
Front row kneeling: Greg Barroso, Anna Haskins, and Christian Maribona, Standing: Bob Bernreuter, Sr. Penny Smith OP (Certification Instructor), Carol Stephens, Mona Clark, DRE Ida Roberts, Sue Barroso, Richard Jabour, and Lana Jabour.

photo by BJBernreuter

# *Ministries of St. Mary  Star of the Sea in Action*

photo by BJBernreuter

## New Beginnings

For 25 years Jean Maun, shown with her husband and helper Jim Maun, has directed the services of New Beginnings. The ministry evolved from the Florida State Respect for Life foundation. This ministry serves the needs of new mothers, helping to insure a good and healthy start for their babies. The Catholic School gets involved each year with service projects to help sort out the clothes, car seats, swings, and other items provided by the ministry.          photo by BJBernreuter

### On the right:
## The Bereavement Group

**Velma Christian and Noni Sanchez are trained counselors who offer support and can assist with planning the Funeral Mass**
**They meet Thursday nights at 7:00 PM at the Spiritual Renewal Center.**
photo by BJBernreuter

## Faculty of St. Mary Star of the Sea Basilica School

L to R: Heidi Hemmesch, Prin. Beth Harris, Danielle Gould, VP Brother Bud Luks, Cindy Hoeffer, Rachael Ambrose, Monica Allen, Gene Drum, Beth Kilroe, Maggie Quintana, Sidney Jones, Ashley Paluch, Kelly Koenig, Erin Luciani, and Eileen Dolan-Heitlinger.

**Photo courtesy of St. Mary Star of the Sea collection**

# Ministries of St. Mary Star of the Sea in Action

**Boy Scout Troop 578 sponsored by the Knights of Columbus** Photo courtesy of Greg Barroso

**Grupo Jesus Bible Study for young Hispanics.**

They meet Thursday nights at 8:00 PM at the Spiritual Renewal Center.
photo by BJBernreuter

On the right:
**Spanish Bible Study**
They meet Thursday nights at 7:30 PM at the Spiritual Renewal Center.
photo by BJBernreuter

On the left:
**Star of the Sea Outreach Mission**

5640 McDonald Ave. on Stock Island. Providing food and clothing to the needy. Also information on Spanish Religious Ed., social service organizations, referral programs, and counseling.
305-292-3013
photo by BJBernreuter

# Ministries of St. Mary Star of the Sea in Action

Spanish Choir    Photo by BJBernreuter

St. Mary's Choir    Photo by BJBernreuter

Children's Choir    Photo by Tom Oosterhoudt

Perpetual Adoration Committee    Photo by Iris Bernreuter

Children's Choir
Photo by BJBernreuter

# Memories of Years Gone By

St. Francis Xavier Altar Boys
St. Mary Star of the Sea collection

1971 MIHS Mariners Football
David Pellico, Timothy Romero,
Theresa Dion, and Robert Goodreau
Charles Malby Jr. collection photo by Bob Cain

1971 MIHS Mariners Basketball
State Runner-up Champions
Charles Malby Jr. collection

Coach Bill Zumberis and the MIHS Mariners, 1971 State Runner-up - 1972 State Champions
Charles Malby Jr. collection

Remarks 2766-X

Piedad L. Parra, July 3rd. 1940
(Worker's full name and date)

HISTORICAL RECORDS SURVEY
CHURCH INVENTORY FORM: 1939

Records not available for inventory

(Fill in each item, or state in items for which information is not available, sources contacted in attempting to secure information.)

1. County___Monroe___  2. City or town___In Key West___

3. Exact name of church___Church of St. Mary Star of the Sea___

4. Street address, R.F.D. route, Highway Number and No. of miles N.,S.,E., or W.
   of nearest town___Division and Windsor Lane Sts.___

5. Race of membership___White___  6. Language of Services___Latin___

7. Denomination (full title)___Roman Catholic___

8. Names and locations of denominational bodies with which church is connected
   (national, state, district, etc. - in descending order of importance)
   
   ___National - Apostolic Delegate to the United States, Washington, D.C.___
   
   ___State   - Diocese of St. Augustine, Florida.___
   
   ___District - None.___

9. Date church organized___1840___  10. Dates of lapse, or date defunct___None___

11. Is church incorporated?___Yes___  12. If so, give date of incorporation___Unknown___

13. Original name of church (if name has changed) and date of change___Same___

14. Name of local parent church (if any) from which organized or split___None___

15. Information on all previous buildings used for services, since organization,
    specifying location and dates used. On October 10, 1846 a priest from Habana
    Cuba celebrated High Mass in the City Hall. First Catholic Church
    erected on a lot on Duval St. near Eaton St. this church burned
    down in 1901, then in 1904 a lot was bought on Division St. which
    at present is located the present church.

JUL 9 1940

**Exhibit A**

180

16. (a) Date present building erected 1904 (b) Date dedicated by this church 1852

(c) Date consecrated by this church _____ (d) If unable to give (b) or (c),

give date of first service of this church in building 1852 (e) If this

building remodelled, give date None (f) Give dates of any additions Giving a new coat of paint at present and other repair

17. (a) Description, architecture (if any definite style), material used, color, form of building (square, T-shaped, etc.) _____

~~Cornerstone, Bell, Pipe Organ, 1 Memorial Window, Altar Service,~~

Gothic Concrete, Natural, T-shaped.

(b) Special features, as cornerstone, art glass or memorial windows, bell, pipe organ, famous paintings, altar service, etc. _____

Cornerstone, Bell, Pipe Organ, 1 Memorial Window Altar Service.

18. Official title of clergyman (rector, priest in charge, pastor, etc.) Rector

19. (a) First settled clergyman Rev. J. N.Brogar Dates of tenure 1852-54

Education Jesuits education

(b) Earliest known clergyman _____ Dates of tenure _____
(If item a is unascertainable)

Education _____

(c) Present clergyman Rev. Patrick J. Kelleher, S.J. Dates of tenure 1939--
(or last clergyman of a defunct church)

Address Division & Windsor Lane Sts.

Education Jesuits education.

20. Unpublished historical sketches (author, title, period covered, date written, location - note if written in one of church record books) _____

None.

21. Published histories, historical sketches, or directories (author, title, publisher, place and date of publication, no. of pages, location) _____

A Historical sketch of the St. Mary Star of the Sea was

published during a benefit frolic. Title; Souvenir Program of the

Benefit Frolic; Author, Father P.J. Kelleher,S.J.; Published May 25,

1940 at Key West, 10 Pages.

**Exhibit B**

# Bibliography

## Records and Manuscript Sources

*Architectural Analysis of St. Mary Star of the Sea Church*, Tom Pope, Key West, 2011.

Archives of Diocese of Savannah, Savannah, Ga.

Archives Sisters of St. Joseph, St. Augustine, Fla. (*Brief History of the Churches of the Diocese of Saint Augustine Florida, Part Six*, Imprimatur June 1923, Abby Press Saint Leo, Florida)

Archives of Saint Leo Abbey, St. Leo, Fla.

Congressional Series Set: 56th Congress, 1st Session, Senate, Document #221, *Report of the Commission Appointed by the President to Investigate the Conduct of the War Department in the War with Spain*, pg. 1937, Washington, Government printing office,

Deeds Summary of Monroe County Courts, Key West, Fla.

*Dictionnaire Biographique du Clergé Canadien- Français Les Anciens*

Fathers of Mercy, South Union, KY.

*Golden Anniversary Program 1949*, Key West, Fla.

Historic Structure Report, Bender & Delaune Architects, P.A., Key West, Fla.

History of St. Mary Star of the Sea, Florence Fuller, additions & corrections: Ray Blazevic, Key West, Fla.

Jesuit Seminary & Mission Bureau, New Orleans, LA.

*Key West in World War II*, A History of the Naval Station and Naval Operating Base 1945 by Lt. Cmdr. J.P. Mickler, USNR

Letter from Dorothy M. Beaver, Aug. 1982

Light of Christ 20th Year Anniversary Celebration program, April 16, 1993, Key West, Fla.

Mary Immaculate High School Development Fund Program, December 1969

Records from the Office of the Chancellor, Archdiocese of Miami, Miami, Fla.

Research and Interviews by Sister Mary Pat Vandercar, Key West, Fla.

Reverend George W. Cummings, Citrus Springs, Fl. (Letter of Fr. LaRocque held in his possession for 60 years.)

*Saint Mary Star of the Sea Catholic Church Key West, Florida, Sesquicentennial (150 Years) 1846-1996*, Bob J. Bernreuter, 1996.

Saint Mary Star of the Sea Parish 1852-1943, Compiled from Historical Documents, Key West, Fla.

Service Central Dex Archives SNJM, Longueuil, Quebec.

Seventh Census of the United States 1850, J.D.B DeBow, Superintendent of the United States.

Sisters of the Holy Names of Jesus and Mary, SNJM Chronicles, New York Province, Montreal, Can.

Sisters of the Holy Names of Jesus and Mary, SNJM Chronicles, Oregon Province, Marylhurst, Or.

*Souvenir Program of the Benefit Frolic, 1940,* Rev. P.Kelleher, S.S., Key West, Fla.

## Magazines

The Columbia, April, 1995

The Overseas Advertizer 200th, Key West, FL. April 1976

## Newspapers

Florida Times- Union, Sept. 24, 1901

Key West Citizen, Oct. 24, 1938

Key West Citizen, 1963
Key West Citizen, April 22, 1968
Key West Citizen, Oct. 24, 1968
Key West Citizen, Feb. 20, 1972
Key West Citizen, Nov. 27, 1977
Key West Citizen, July 13, 1979
Key West Citizen, Sept. 5, 1980
Key West Citizen, Feb. 25, 2011
The Florida Catholic, Apr. 28, 1995
The Florida Catholic, Jan. 5, 1996
The Miami Daily News Sunday Magazine, Feb. 15, 1948
The Miami Herald, April 23, 1968
The Miami Herald, 1970
The Miami Herald, 1972
The Miami Herald, July 1, 1982
The Miami Herald, Sept. 6, 1987
The Miami Metropolis, 1905
The Miami Metropolis, August 24, 1905
The Milwaukee Journal, August 18, 1962
The News Tribune, Fort Pierce, Fl, November 2, 1972
The Voice, Dec. 9, 1977
The Voice, Oct. 7, 1983
The Voice, Jan. 5, 1996

St. Mary Star of the Sea collection

St. Mary Star of the Sea collection

## Internet

Archdiocese of Miami, www.miamiarch.org
Diocese of Havana, www.diocese of Havana, Cuba
Diocese of Santiago, www.diocese of Santiago, Cuba
Dominican Pioneer, Pacifist Preacher & Martyred Missionary, http://www.domcentral.org/trad/cancerop.htm
Fathers of Mercy, www.fathersofmercy.com/about/history
Fr. Seamus Ward, http://keysnews.com/node/30098
Historic Florida Indians, Jerry Wilkinson, www.keyshistory.org/histindians.html
McSherry, Patrick, Torpedo Boat Winslow, www.spanamwar.com/winslow.htm
Wilkinson, Jerry, History of Key West, www.keyshistory.org/keywest.html
The Cathedral Basilica of Saint Augustine, www.thefirstparish.org
St. Michael Church named minor basilica, www.pnj.com/.../St-Michael-church-named-minor-basilica-by-Vatica...
Instituto San Carlos, http://www.institutosancarlos.org/history.php

## Books

Brevard, Caroline Mays, *A History of Florida*. New York: American Book Company, 1919.
Browne, Jefferson B., *Key West: The Old and the New*. St. Augustine: The Record Company, 1912.
*Called to Cast Fire*, Trans. Francis Allison SNJM, from the French, out of print.
Gannon, Michael V., *The Cross in the Sand*. Gainesville: University of Florida Press, 1965.

George, Paul S., *The Gesu in Miami: A Story of God's People in a Subtropical Metropolis, 1896–2006.* Hialeah: Fort Dallas Press, 2006.

Herrera, Antonio de, *Historia general de los hechos de los Castellanos en las islas y tierra firme del Mar Oceano.* 4 vols, Madrid: 1601-1615.

Hudson, Charles, *Knights of Spain, Warriors of the Sun.* Athens: University of Georgia Press, 1997

*St. Joseph Edition of The New American Bible.* New York: Catholic Book Publishing Co., 1987.

Langley, Wright & Joan, *Key West & The Spanish- American War.* Key West: Langley Press Inc. 1998.

McEwan, Bonnie G., *The Spanish Missions of La Florida.* Gainesville: University Press of Florida, 1993.

Maloney, Walter C., *A Sketch of the History of Key West, Florida.* Facsimile of 1876 edition, Gainesville: University of Florida Press, 1968.

Maloney, Walter H., *Our Catholic Roots, Old Churches East of the Mississippi.* Indiana: Our Sunday Visitor Publishing Division, 1992.

McNally, Michael J., *Catholicism in South Florida 1868-1968.* Gainesville: University of Florida Press, 1982.

Parks, Pat, *The Railroad That Died At Sea*, Key West: The Langley Press, 1986.

Vega, Garcilaso de la, *The Florida of the Inca.* Trans. John G. Varner and Jeannette J. Varner, Austin: University of Texas Press, 1962.

Viele, John, *The Florida Keys A History of the Pioneers.* Sarasota: Pineapple Press, Inc.,1996.

Viele, John, *The Florida Keys Volume 2, True Stories of the Perilous Straits.* Sarasota: Pineapple Press, Inc., 1999.

White, Louise V. and Smiley, Nora K., *History of Key West Today and Yesterday.* St. Petersburg, Great Outdoors Publishing Co., 1959.

Writers Program, Work Projects Administration in the State of Florida, *A Guide to Key West.* New York: Hastings House Publishers,1949.

Convent Gates: the graduate opens the gates for a new generation in 1947.
St. Mary Star of the Sea collection

Photo courtesy of *The Florida Catholic*

185

## About the Author

### Bob J. Bernreuter

A sixth generation "Conch", Bob grew up in Key West during the fifties and sixties, graduating from St. Joseph's School in 1960 and from Key West High School in 1964. He lives in Key West, Florida, with his wife Iris. Both are 1968 graduates of Florida State University. Bob received a B.A. in Speech & Drama with a minor in English, and his wife Iris, a degree in Education. After college he served ten years active duty in the U.S. Air Force, as an instructor pilot. He completed three tours of duty, flying the KC-135, in Southeast Asia during the Vietnam War. Bob, a Fourth Degree Knight of Columbus, has taught religious education at St. Mary Star of the Sea since 1987. For the past three decades he has been writing stories for his four children, grandchildren, and students; some have been published in the local papers and others freely distributed. **THE GIFT** was his first commercially published book.

Our web site: **www.keywestpublishingllc.com**
This book is available at St. Mary Star of the Sea Gift Store and through all major bookstores. Retailers can order through:
**Baker & Taylor Books - Quality Books Inc. - BWI - Emery Pratt Company**

*Key West*
PUBLISHING, LLC